Social Media, Social Mess?

AUTHORED AND ILLUSTRATED BY

RASHMI SANDERS

ISBN: 9781710627879

Independently published

DEDICATION

This book is dedicated to anyone who has ever read a post on social media and felt they haven't got enough, felt left out of the fun, felt fat at the sight of skinny photos or simply sad because someone didn't say something nice. You're not alone..

WHATS ON THE AGENDA

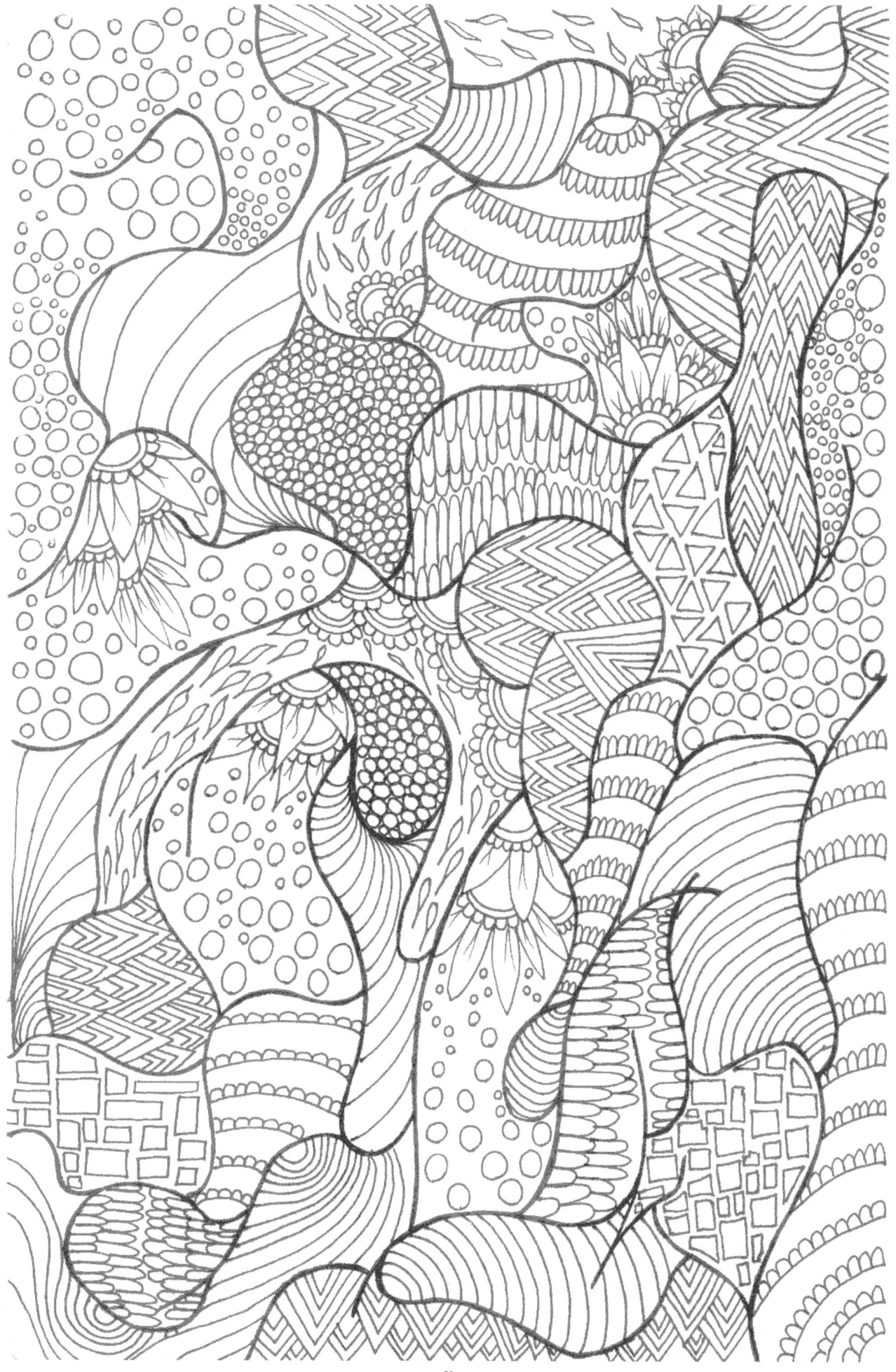

DISCLAIMER

Before anyone decides to sue me, I just wanted to be clear about something. This book is not meant to offend anyone and is based on my opinion and mine alone. Any stories that have been told have been anonymized and anyone who I have quoted, I have asked their permission.

The big issue is that I don't stop thinking. All day and all night, I think about people, careers, interactions, behaviours, life, kids, husbands, relationships and anything in between.

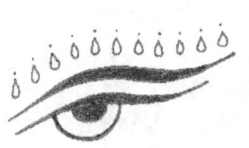

"How do I motivate X?"
"Why do my kids behave so differently? "
"Urgh!!! Damn scales I need to go back on plan. "
"Tomorrow I need to do a, b, c, d.... "
"Oh hubby is off to China I need the dates to ensure I'm close to home. "
"Is my Mum ok? "
"I need to call my Dad. "
"Shit, there's been an accident on the M1, I should warn my brother."

Drawing is the only way for me to calm those thoughts and put them on paper. Some people write journals, some talk to friends and family, but I draw. It is one of three places I feel most content. The other places involve being with my family or at work. Maybe a fourth would include eating at my local Turkish restaurant.

So basically, there is no need to get your knickers in a twist. Please don't take the comments too seriously but I hope you enjoy colouring in the artwork.

Additionally, an equal percentage of the profits will be going to three charities

Mind: Looking after the mental well-being of the nation.
Alzheimer's UK: Future research into memory loss and support for affected families and patients.
Macmillan UK: Support for families and patients with cancer.

The intention of this book is to help people think about how they use social media and the manner in which it can affect our thinking and so it feels only right to use some of the profits to help a charity that can support progression in this area.

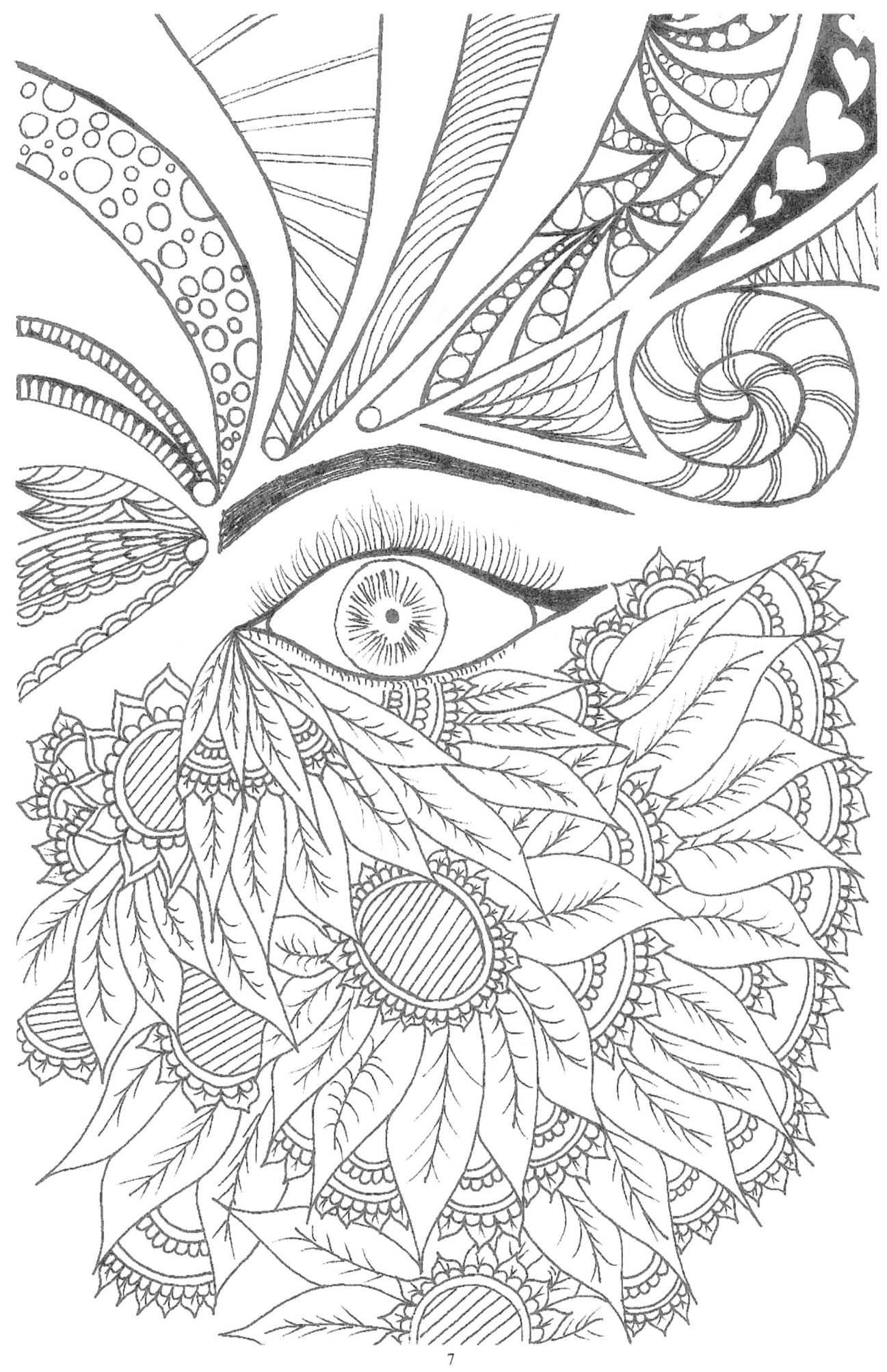

INTRODUCTION

Subsequent to publishing the last book, the biggest question I was asked was "How long does each doodle take you?" I would say that the last book "A Working Mum's Mind" had about 150 hours worth of art work.

This colouring book is very different. As with everything in life, the more you practice, the better your skill, but this takes time. The artwork over the coming pages has taken approximately 300 hours and this is simply because I have tried to be more intricate, worked with fine liners and been far more critical of my work. Each piece of work can take between three to ten hours.

There has also been additional hours of research on subjects such as the link between social media and mental health, along with reading lots of clinical trials looking at this very topic. I'm not saying I'm an expert now but I have learned so much along the way. We are now talking about mental well-being on a daily basis and social media plays a large role in this. Whether it's positive or negative, we have to acknowledge that for some, social media is a saviour and yet for others it is the thing that will make them want to question each aspect of their life. More and more studies are being conducted into the impact it has, and overall, it's not looking great. When having an opinion on what I have seen, I have wanted to ensure that I understand the facts and figures behind the thoughts to see if I have made the right or wrong assumption. Year on year, the number of people using social media increases, and with this comes a responsibility to use it wisely and cause no harm.

The financial cost of this book is the sum total of about a million coffees at the local coffee shop where I now know the team in Costa pretty well, along with pens and sketch books (other coffee shops are available before someone pipes up).

But the one thing that was not acknowledged in the last book was the sheer number of hours my husband has put in to ensure that the publishing of this book is done correctly, not to mention the correction of some of my errors when the table wobbled and my pen scrawled across the page. The digital aspect is my biggest weakness and so without him, these books would never happen and the money I have raised for charity through the sale of them would not be possible.

So to you my Big Man, I say thank you. For your support, your corrections and your listening ears to my "Rash's Rants". Thank you.

For everyone else reading this, a sincere thank you for purchasing the book. I truly hope you enjoy colouring in the doodles. Please don't forget to join in on Instagram and tag each of your coloured pages using the hashtag at the bottom of the pages.

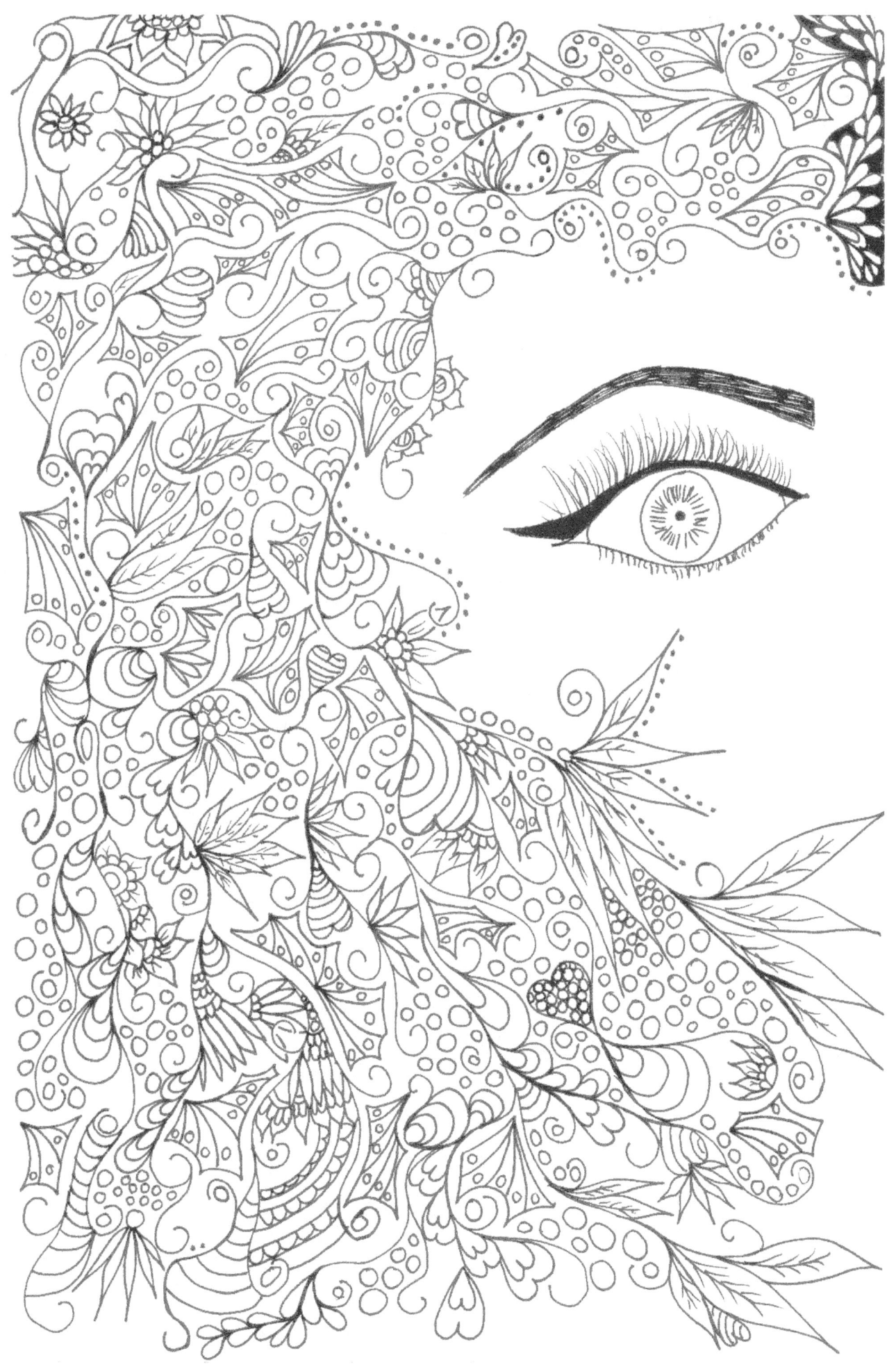

SHOW THE WORLD

Despite social media having been around for quite some time now, statistics published in the Global Digital Report 2019, show that year on year the use of social media grows by a staggering nine percent.

We have never been more connected than we are right now. When discussing this book with a dear friend of mine, Kristen, she said "Social media provides us with unlimited opportunities to present ourselves to the world". People have multiple accounts for the different parts of their lives, whether it is Linked In for business, Instagram for hobbies, Facebook for social and others for other. Some days I'm not even sure if or how we are built to actually cope with it mentally.

Security is also a big issue. In 2017 I took the chance to learn about social media security settings for all of my accounts as I was concerned that members of the public could see pictures of my children and so I ensured all my settings disabled this from happening. It also meant that any future employers could not see anything from my personal life as this is no concern of anyone else's in my opinion.

However, have you ever typed your name and residing city into google? This is the moment you will see what is publicly available for anyone to see about you. Possible outcomes include:

- Address or previous residence
- Linked in profiles and therefore employment details
- Link to Facebook and Instagram accounts
- Photos that are public
- Charity events and even links to when you have donated on certain sites
- News articles, "The Good, the Bad and the Ugly"
- Links to your partners social media accounts and sometimes friends when you have been tagged
- And much more.

So, with "unlimited opportunities to present ourselves", as Kristen said, and with an ever growing population of social media users, what do you really want to show the world?

When you can't quite seem to get the job you want, is it possible that your employer has seen photos of you out plastered with your friends, or have you been tagged in a political post that may cause conflict professionally?

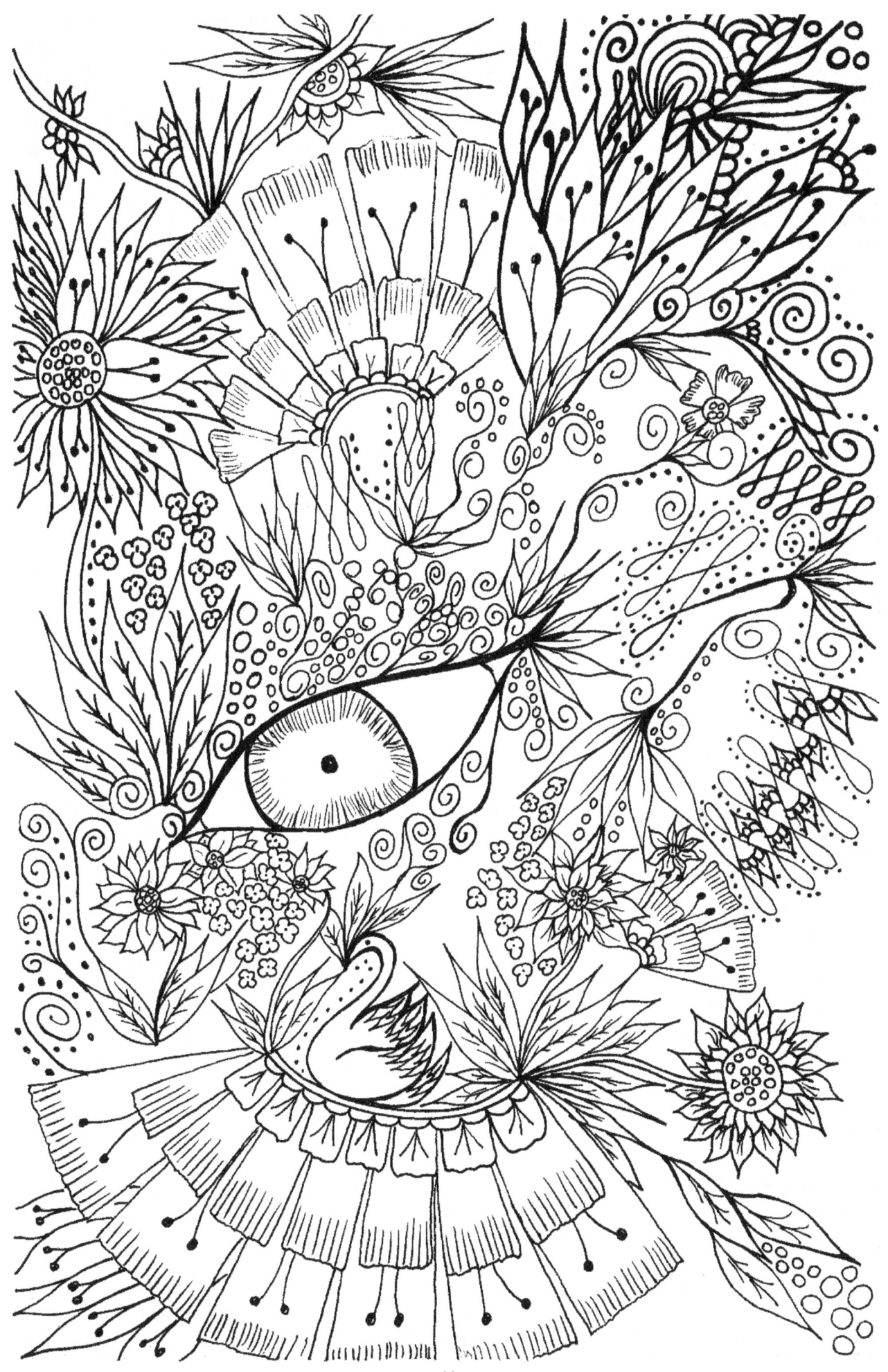

I met a young lady once who spoke to me openly about how she felt in her career at the time. Ella told me that she felt discriminated against due to being a woman and wanted to be taken seriously. I decided to be honest with her and told her I would come back to her. I went away and did some internet research, most lovingly termed as "face stalking". Ok so here goes on what I saw:

Half naked modelling photos
Massive cleavage and pouting in every photo
Grinding on a nightclub dance floor
Linked in profile with six jobs in the last 22 months
Photos of her in bed crying because she has anxiety and depression.

Her internet profile screamed of someone who would call in sick weekly, someone who is mentally unwell and would need a huge amount of support and someone who potentially has a second job in modelling and therefore may not take the role she is applying for seriously.

I wouldn't wish mental health problems on my worst enemy and it's great to talk about it but is this what you want to be known for when your aim is to go further and you are looking for opportunities?

If you are comfortable with your profile content, that's a great thing but just keep an eye out for the security settings. I had a significant breach of security this year and a member of the public stalked me on both Instagram and Facebook. I felt extremely let down, and to know my photos had been viewed by someone without my permission really upset me. The stalking was aimed at myself but that individual went on to see my children too.

Suffice to say, I went through everything again but I wouldn't want this happening to anyone else. Your data is your data. Don't allow anyone to use it against you.

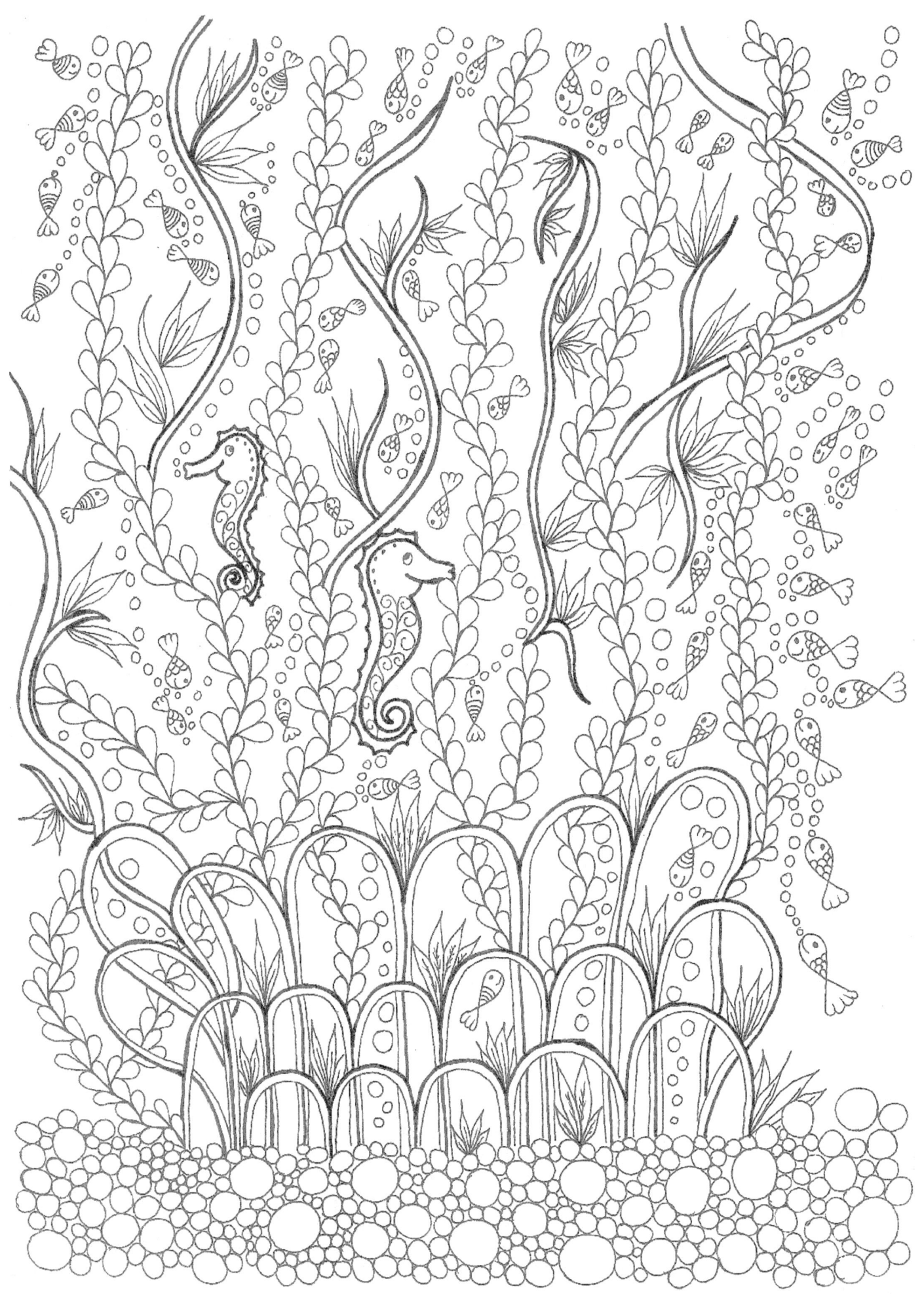

BUDDING BUSINESS

People have the ability to share so much on social media and a new business is one of those things. How incredible is it that we can start a page and ask our friends to share and like and it costs nothing but time?

However, people seem to fall into two camps on this.
1. Willing to share and invite people to join the new budding business
2. Never willing to share for various reasons

According to a business news page, the top things a new business owner should do on Facebook include:
A) Post regularly
B) Be social and include people
C) Leverage friends and fans of your page
D) Promote your page

Now those in camp one, in my experience are people who are encouraging of others doing well. Generally speaking, they like to see people happy and they want to be helpful and feel enjoyment from their friends and family doing well. And so as a result, the advice above is possible for them to be successful.

However, we have those in camp two. There are many who don't share a business page to help a friend out but there are multiple reasons for this. Some don't wish to be affiliated with another company, some just think the business idea is just ridiculous or even goes against a belief they have about the products or services on offer, but some are just simply a little jealous. And then of course there are those that are just tired of "yet another small business" or a "new rival business".

From the other side of the coin, the person starting the page is possibly someone who would like to change their lives and become independent from their current job, or even do something to bring them back into the workplace. Some of my friends have stated that they simply cannot make ends meet on their current income and therefore need to work on something else that doesn't jeopardize their current job. By not helping them out, we could possibly be hindering something that could make the world of difference to them.

In short, I believe we all have the capability to help someone for no cost, just a little time on social media. We have a chance to make a positive difference using a platform that has the capability of reaching thousands in minutes. Why would you not want to help them?

After all, how many times have we seen people asking "Anyone recommend a good plumber?" Or "Decorator needed, all recommendations welcome". We all need help every so often and the small business owners out there need the business to survive.

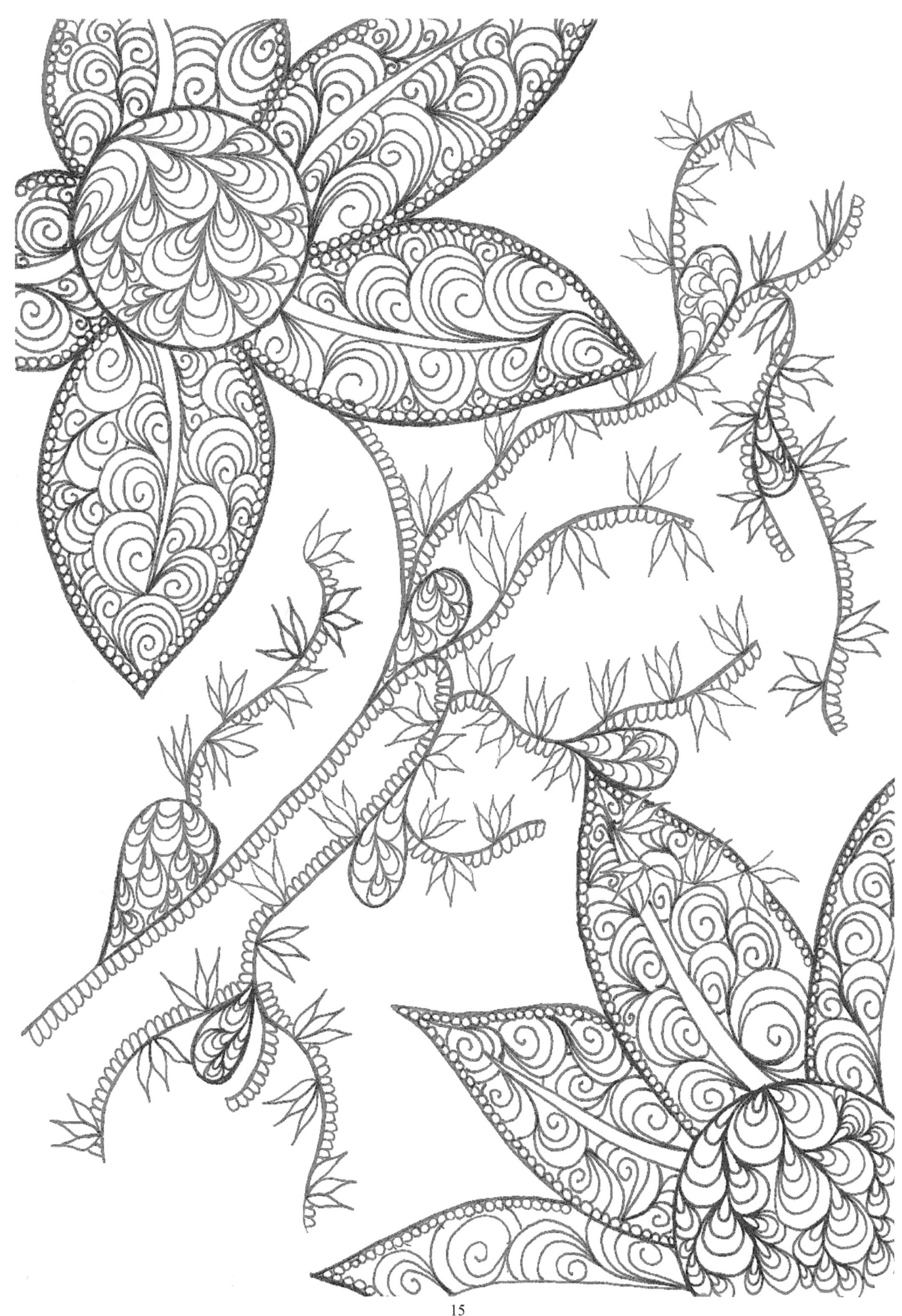

SOCIAL BUTTERFLY

So one week you see a post with someone out with their friends.

The next week they are out again

The same the week after.

Makes you sick doesn't it? I'm sat indoors with a jigsaw, watching Neighbours on a Friday night while some are out dressed up and raring to go. Truth be told by the end of the week I'm so tired I literally cannot he bothered. But yet we are.

Then next thing you know you're organizing an evening out and the same person says

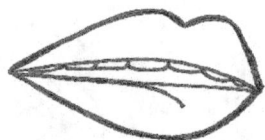

"Can we go low key? I can't afford a lot at the moment". So let's analyse this:

Thoughts include:

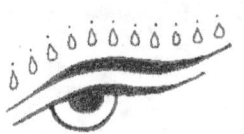

"You've been out every week with your other mates and spent a load of money on your weekends away but you save the cheap meal out for me? Mmmm"
"Not a problem. I'm relaxed anyway. "
"Why didn't you invite me to that event, that event or that event? "
"Yeah whatever"
"Hold on. Just stop thinking and say yes"

In reality, (as an example) the first night posted was a work do. The second night was a family meal paid for by Mum and Dad and the weekend away was actually saved up for.

But social media tells us everyone is out having an incredible time and we are dull because we are at home. However, it's not always as it seems. Many didn't even want to go out. Lots of people even end up in arguments while enjoying a so called evening drink and some save going out for when there is a big celebration. And why not?!!!

As for those of us staying at home doing the knitting and jigsaws, I say that's cool too.

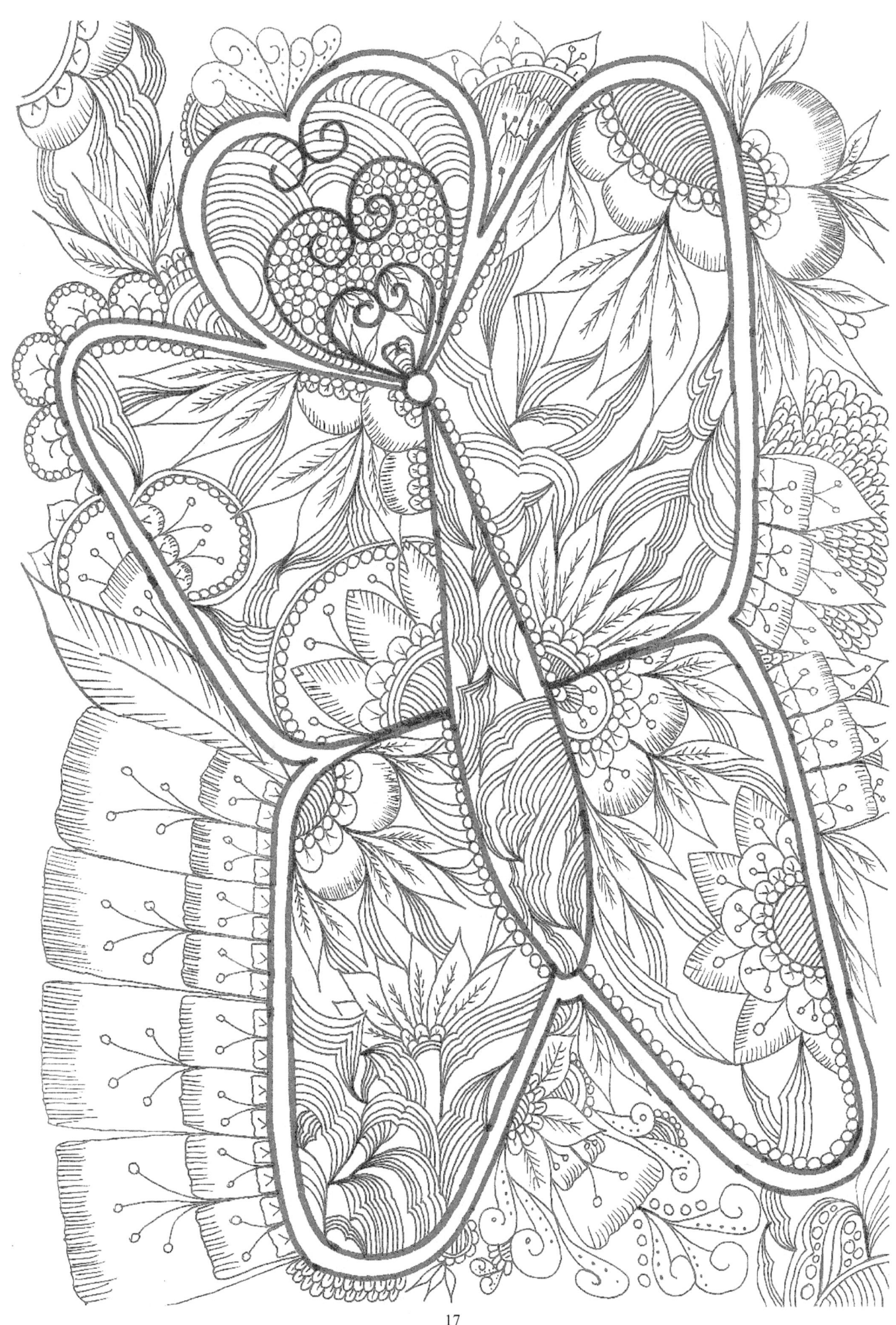

SILENCE IS GOLDEN

Really? Silence is golden? My fat arse it's "golden". In social media terms silence speaks volumes. To me, it says one of a few things about the silenced individual.

Random post……Responses available:
Like, love, statement. It's not rocket science or time consuming.

Silenced individual, you say to me one of the following:

1. You have unfollowed me because I have bored the life out of you
2. You are jealous
3. You are lazy
4. You are a stalker who is watching all I do.
5. You're a mindless scroller
6. You don't know how to use social media
7. You are hiding from people
8. You've suspended your account
9. You are guilty of doing what "the share" might be talking about
10. You're too busy working.

If people never like the posts or actively use social media, then essentially why are they even on it? Or why are you friends with people that seem to avoid saying anything nice to you? I just don't understand. About three years ago, I decided that social media is a means of communication. To me, communication is a two way process and so if someone does not communicate back in any way, shape or form then there is no point in having them on your media.

I came to see that my posts weren't ever liked by particular people. At first it bothered me but as time went on, I genuinely think I had forgotten these people existed on social media. However, then comes the day when finally one of them hit the like button on something I said. Shocked!! A pig just flew over my house. Let me explain why. During the initial moments when I realized they have nothing nice to say, I was a little weak and sold it to myself that they just don't have time. I told myself not to take it personally or to understand that they may have just unfollowed me. Having this new like now meant that that person had seen my posts all along. They actively chose to ignore me, actively chose to never say anything nice, actively avoided my comments and so and so on.

The good news is that this shock lasted all of about three minutes but after the three minutes I lost respect for that person. Rightly or wrongly, that's what happened. It was the moment I felt that person wasn't nice. I like nice people and we are all human and most of us, like to be liked. For some people though, this is something very difficult to deal with mentally but we have to put things into perspective and ignore it. Hollow likes and attention is just bad for us in my opinion. De-friending, however, is lush. Try it. Great for the soul!

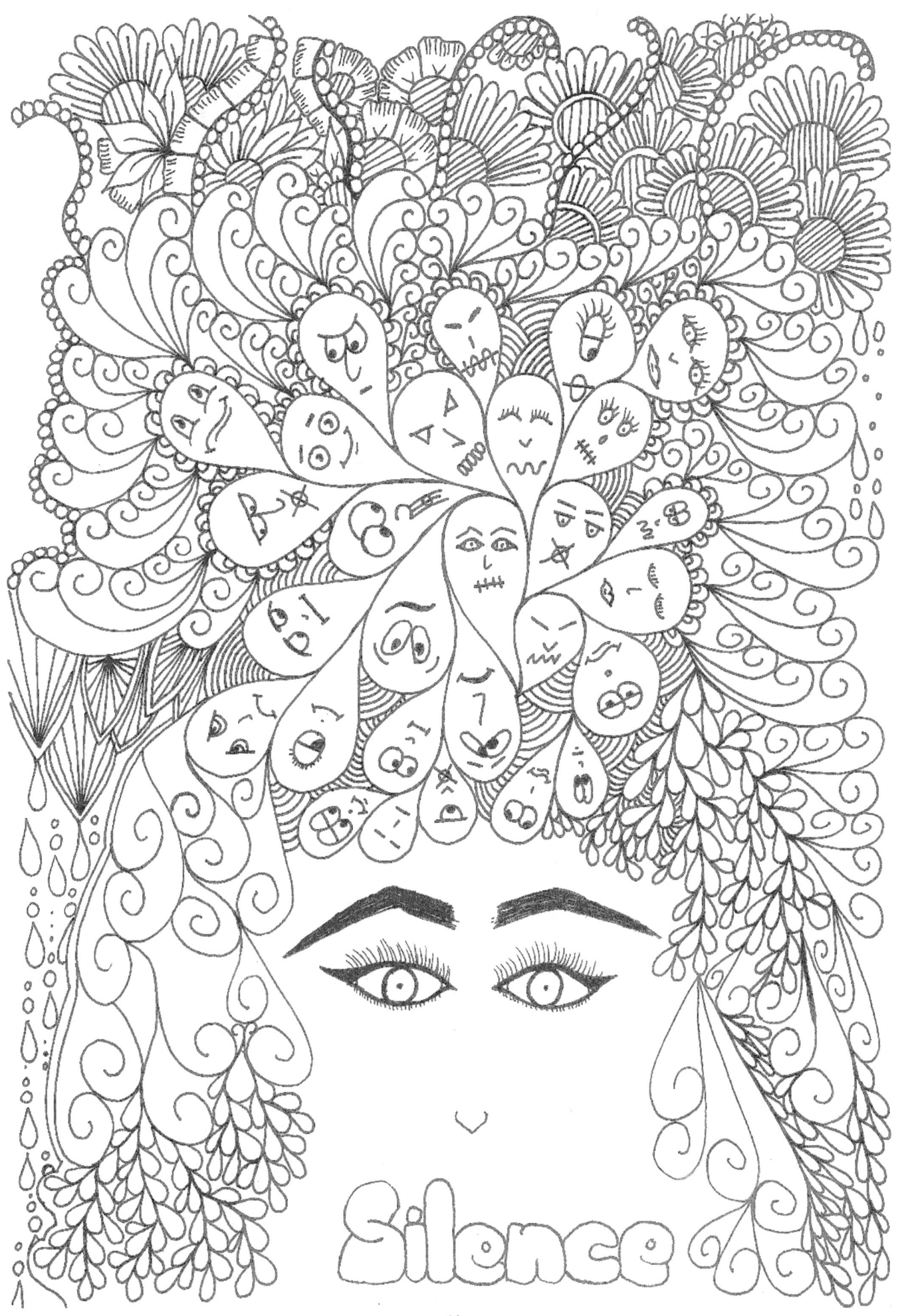

THE GREAT DIVIDE

A dangerous subject to be covered but here goes. A book about how we use social media would not really work if I didn't cover off the Brexit debate.

Now I'm not going into my vote or reasons on this but just my observations of what I have seen over the last three years and I do feel a real sense of upset and anger with regards to this topic. Social media played an extremely heavy role in swaying people's decisions and some of those articles that were shown and shared have now been proven to have been factually incorrect. As a result, is it now possible we have a population of voters who may not have voted the way they did or even choose to abstain from the vote altogether?

The day the results came in, I will never forget the barrage of abuse that was sent out by my own followers and friends towards those who had voted for Brexit. Whatever the result was I promised myself I would be fine either way and would never negate those who voted the opposite way. It is a democracy after all. What shocked me was the blatant use of foul language, insults and assumptions that those people who had voted for Brexit must have been ill educated and have no awareness of the world. That was an extremely wrong assumption.

I even watched one particular person aggressively abusing those who had voted to leave, only for his own brother-in-law to comment and say:

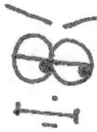 "So me and your father-in-law can f^^k off then shall we?"

Now in fairness that blunder made me howl with laughter as he had only just married into the family two months before!

But in that moment all respect had been lost. Without knowing what family and friends had voted for, many people literally posted to taunt the other side and it wasn't "banter", it was actual nasty comments. Within a 24 hour period, members of the public openly showed their political cards and that paved way for large scale debates over the last three years. Those very debates have led to friends falling out, divides in families, false understanding of what it all means, sharing of memes in which politicians have been accused of all sorts and a whole pile of other problems.

I recently watched an interview with a dating website expert who now has evidence that nearly 60% of his clients will not date someone who voted the opposite way to them in the Brexit vote. We are even closing off our circles of relationships before they have started.

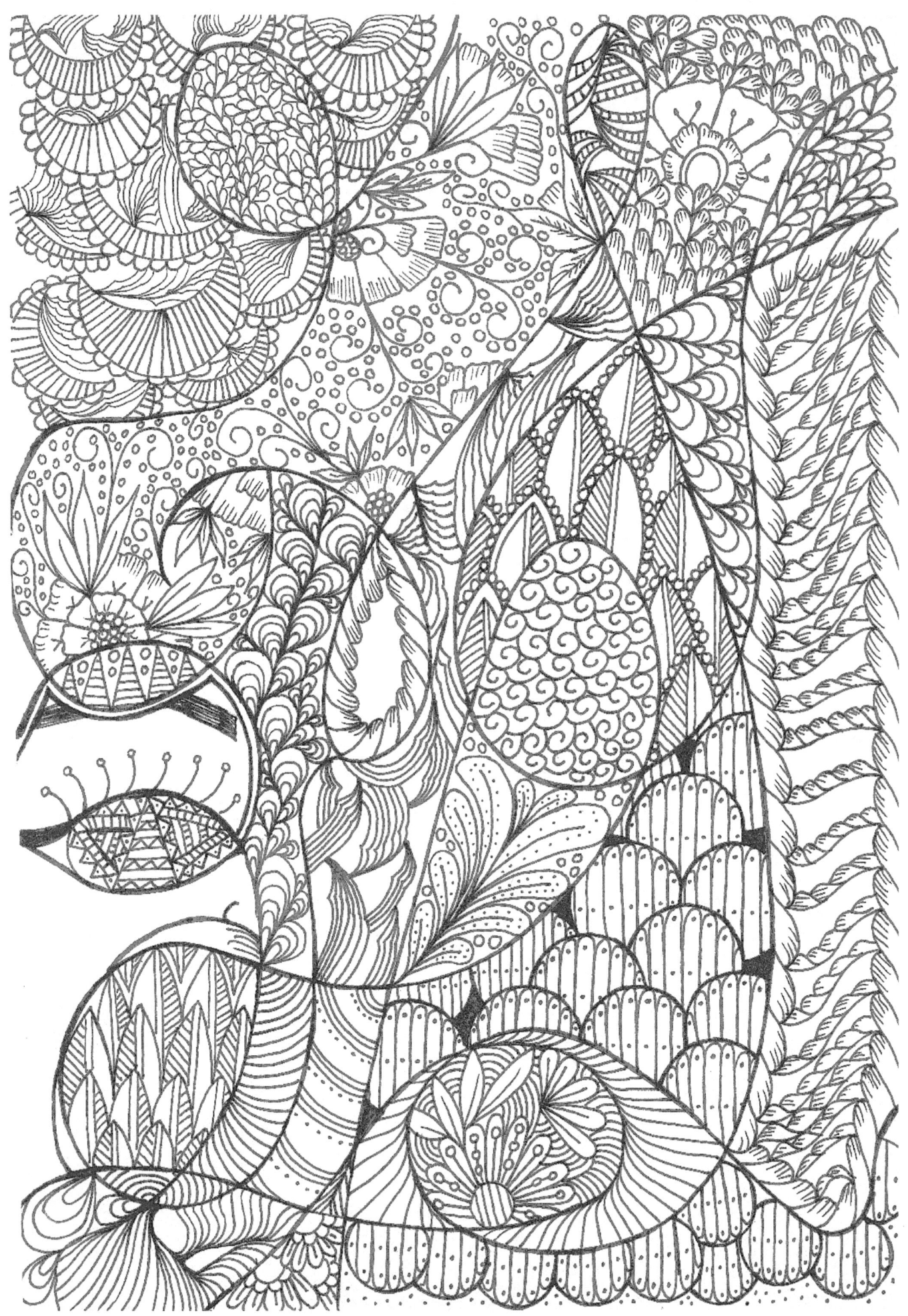

During the Scottish referendum, I asked a colleague of mine how things were on the Scottish team while it was all happening, and I found his response so sad. He said:

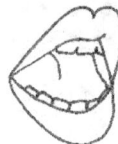

"Rash, we are all divided. I chose not to speak about it but team meetings have been so uncomfortable and the tension is there all the time and it doesn't feel like we are a team anymore".

Such a negative impact on people who had worked together for years and were happy and peaceful. The day the votes came in, I even remember one person posting:

"You bunch of f****g traitors, how could you be so f*****g spineless? You've destroyed this great country".

Really? I don't think so child. Hold your tongue please.

It's not life and death. Is there really any need for people to do this? Don't forget, once you've posted it, it's out there. Besides, I don't know about you but I was always told it was never a good idea to talk about religion, football and politics?

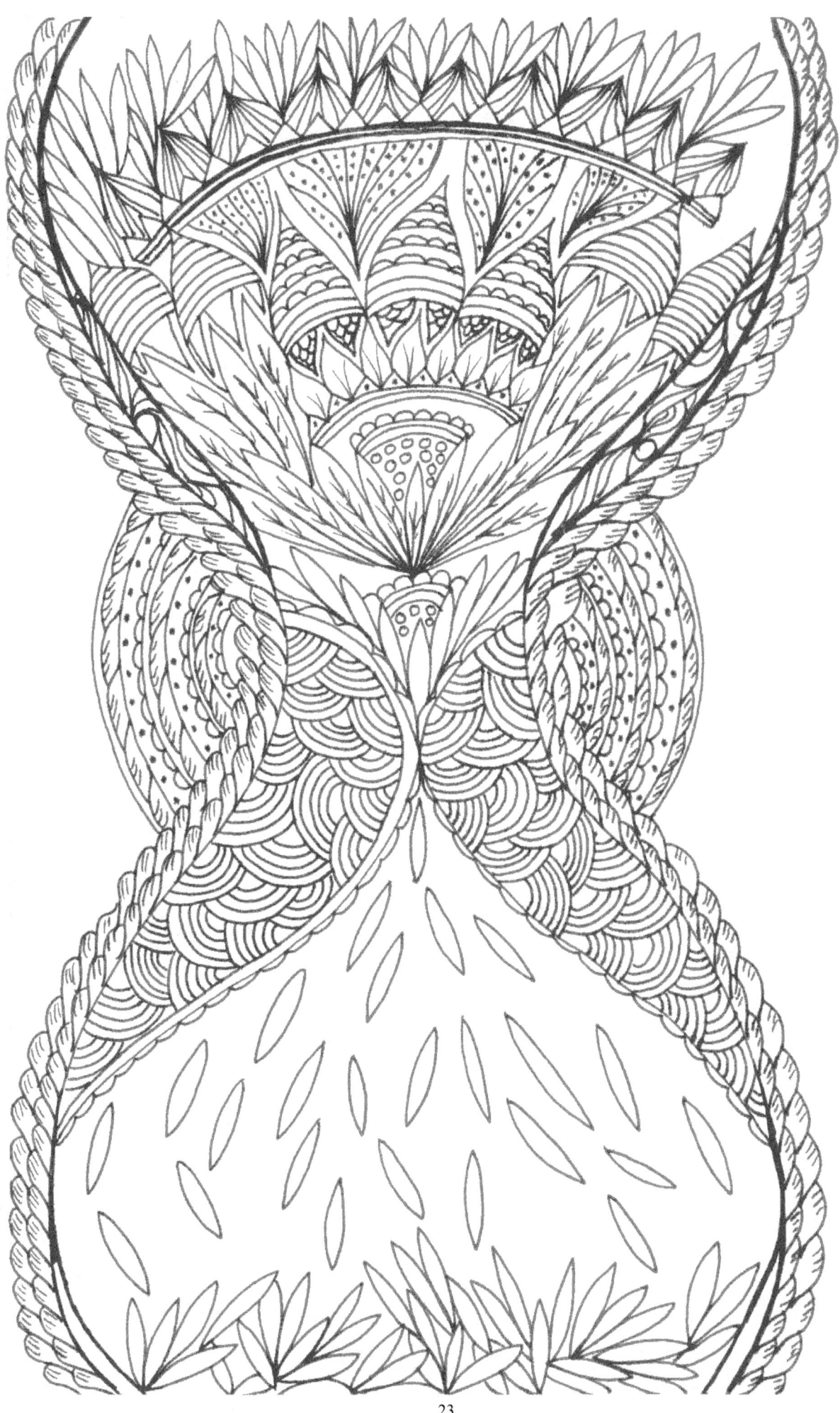

UNITED

Even though we are all different, there are many things on social media that we can all pretty much agree on. I sat down one morning at the coffee shop with my husband and asked:

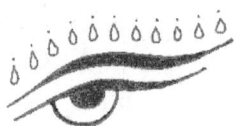

Rash: "What do we all agree on when it come to social media?"

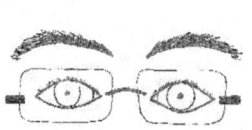

Big Man:
"Funny is funny
Cute fluffy animals are cool
Good looking food makes us hungry
Too many emotional quotes can be annoying
Vague posts irritate people
Great for keeping up with friends and family
The holiday industry would be worse off without it as people's holiday posts make us want to go on holiday
Safety announcements are a positive"

The reason I asked him is because we have the same morals but as people we are incredibly opposite in the way we display our views and so I felt that if we can come up with a list of things that we agree on, it wouldn't be far off.

The problem with "funny is funny" though, is that there is always one person that will take offense. Jokes about hormonal angry women will always have one commenting about how people shouldn't laugh about the menopause, animals dressed in Halloween costumes will always get an accusation of animal cruelty and children throwing the most hilarious strops on camera, always get the mother's brigade shouting that the parent should be concentrating on the child rather than taking a video. Call child protection there is parent who is at whit's end! How dare they be?!

For just one moment, drop the political correctness, stop being offended and see the funny side.

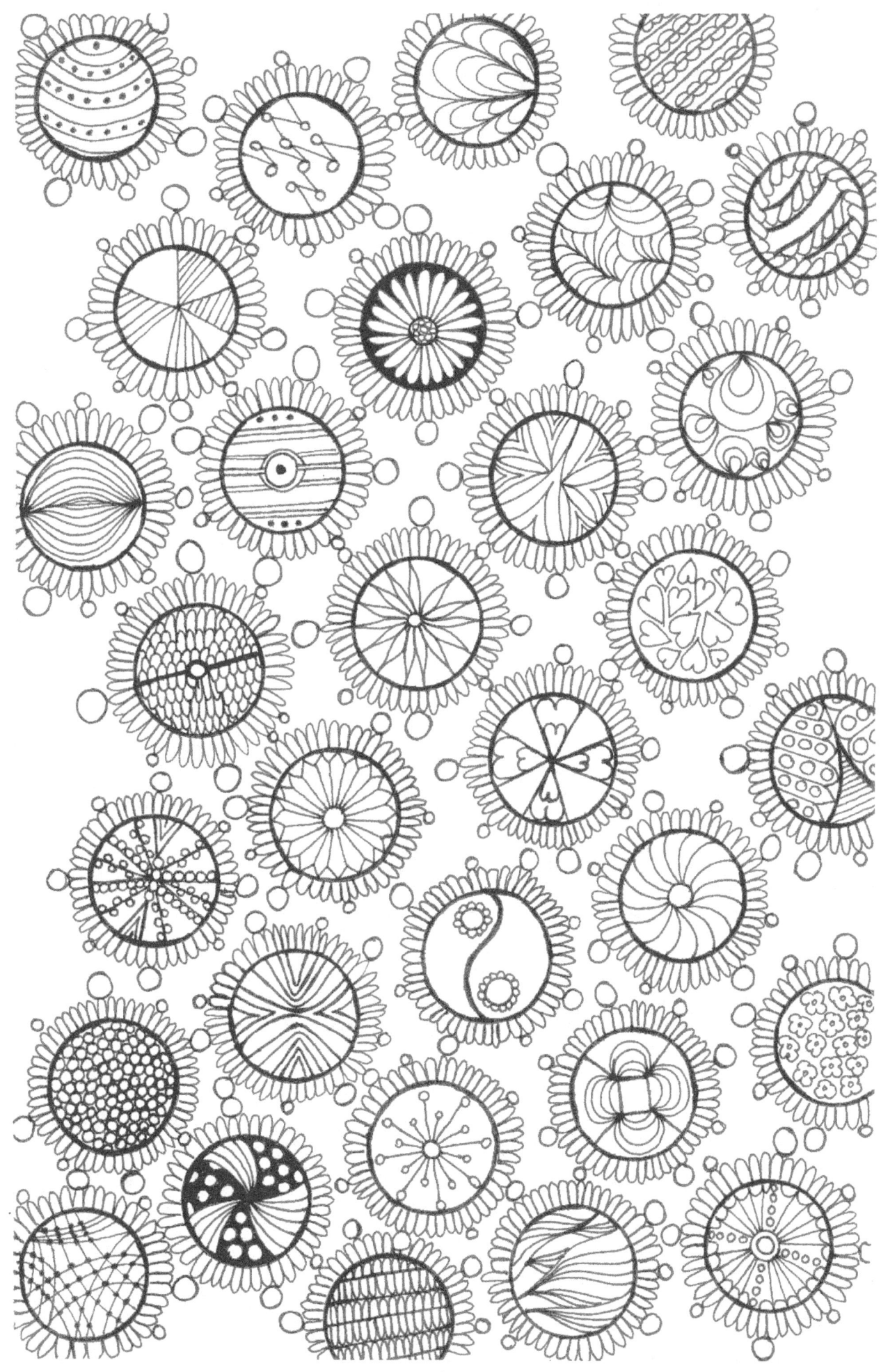

PROFESSIONAL NETWORK

We tend to think of social media for all of our personal life stuff, but there are also those platforms in which we can use for our careers and business, to help us grow. Platforms like Linked In allow us a chance to present our skills in the work place and to an audience that we have tailored through the connections we built up.

In the old days, networking was done in groups and sometimes within very secret ways, such as the Masons, where many business men would get together and discuss their latest projects and help each other out. "You scratch my back, I will scratch yours", if you know what I mean. Nowadays, however, this is quite an old mentality and professional sites give everyone equal opportunities to learn and grow business, skill sets, opportunities and reputation.

There has to be a story though right? So I was on linked in earlier this year, and came across a share from someone who had seen a young man with a billboard on his back. It stated he was a graduate and wanted to look for work and had his CV with him if anyone was interested. Personally, I thought this was a real act of bravery from this very professionally dressed young man at the tube station and so I wanted to encourage him and wish him luck. I decided to comment some words of encouragement:

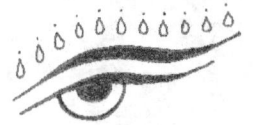
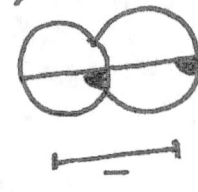

Rash "Big act of bravery right there. I think you will go far and I wish you all the best of luck in the pursuit of your dream job"

Random pillock: "You're obviously another moron who f*****d up and supported Brexit"

Rash: "Hi there, I'm not sure what Brexit has to do with my words of encouragement to this young man. Also, please may I ask you don't swear in replies to my comments. We are on a professional site and I find it cheap and unprofessional"

Random pillock: "You know nothing about me you c**t. Who the f**k do you think you are telling me what to do, you Brexit loving twat!"

At this point I decided to be the bigger person and deleted my comments and the thread, as I would never want to be associated with such behaviour. I felt really angry that someone I had never even met, had sworn at me for no good reason. I still have no idea what Brexit had to do with me wishing this boy good luck! If you do know please let me know through my DM on Instagram @rasheedoodlesaway.

Moral of the story. There are many plonkers out there. Be prepared for the trolls and learn to laugh it off because they don't care what the subject, what the forum or who is watching them. You may or may not want to delete threads like I did, but you have a choice to portray yourself as something specific on different platforms so be aware of what may come your way.

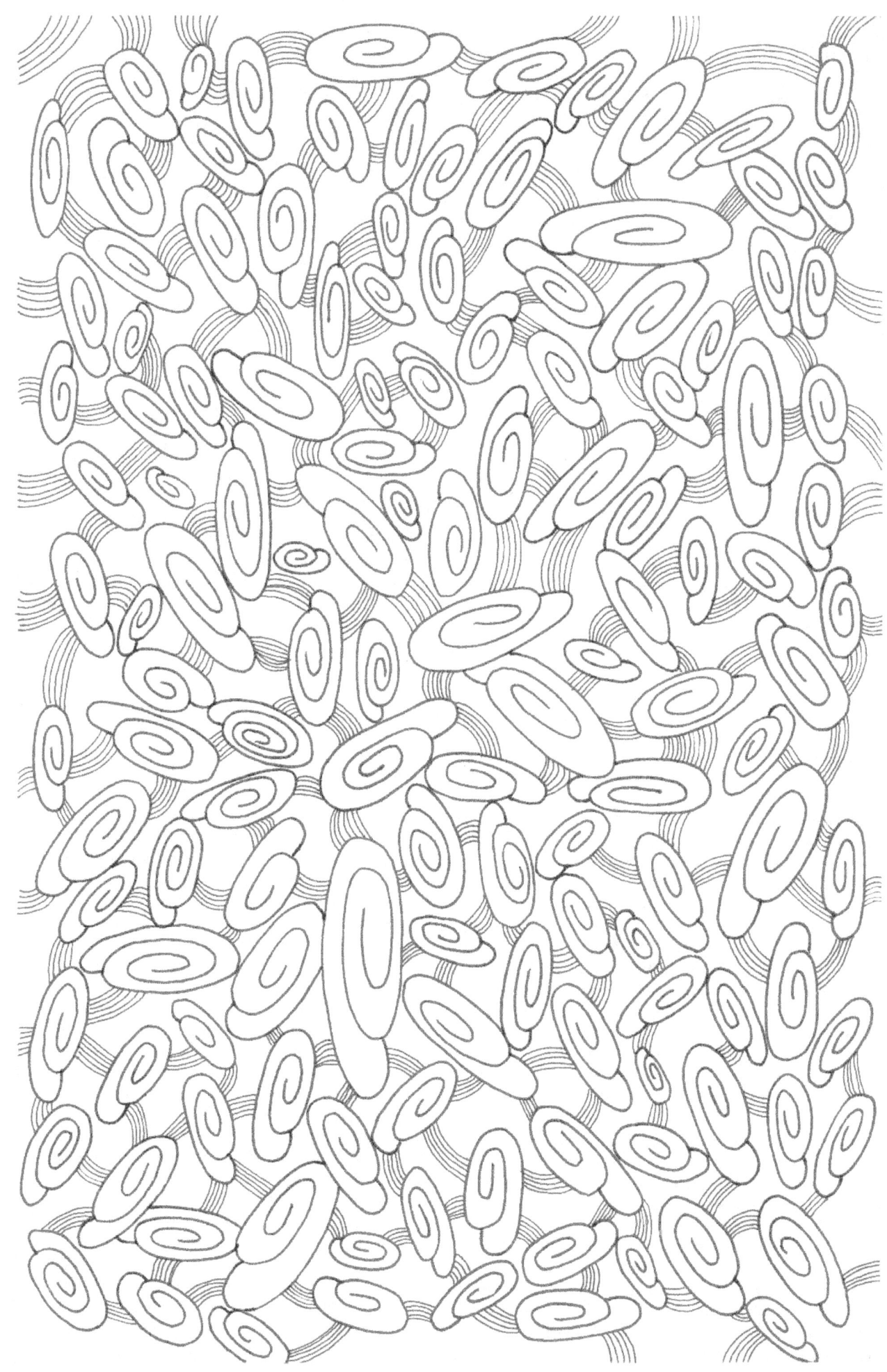

PROFILE PHOTO

I was complemented a lot on my Linked In profile picture when I uploaded it in September of 2018. I had recently gone through a new re-structure at work and some of my team were new to me. I had got it in my thick head that I wanted to look a little softer, so if they looked at my experience on Linked In they would see a person who was approachable, kind and motivating. The reason I had done this is because in the past, a few people have told me that I have a look which shouts "Don't f**k with me". Personally, I find this hilarious. But it is fairly accurate though.

Back to the profile photo…… I was so pleased with it, I decided to upload it to Facebook and Instagram also. My eyes looked lighter in the sun, my hair was wavy, I was wearing nice make-up and ready to go for a nice BBQ at my friend Sophia's house. I had been really missing her and couldn't wait to see her so I made extra effort. I decided that it was a good look to do a softer photo. Here's how it went.

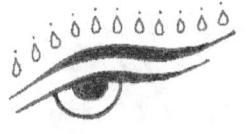

> **Rash**: "Darling I want to change my profile photo on Linked In."
>
> **Big Man**: "Why?"
>
> **Rash**: "Sounds stupid but if anyone in the new team check out my profile, I want them to see a nice approachable manager. I think I look a little bitchy in the other photo. I think it would help if there were trees in the back ground."
>
> **Big Man**: "Your last photo is fine."
>
> **Rash**: "My cheeks are chubbier and it's been five years. They also need to know I'm not a child. And today I'm not wearing bright red lippie so I look a little less harsh."
>
> **Big Man**: "Fine. We have no trees in our garden"
>
> **Rash**: "There are trees over the road."
>
> **Big Man**: "But Rash, the streets rubbish is piled under it for collection. Do you really want to have your photo with a load of rubbish bags? "
>
> **Rash**: "It's fine! Stop being fussy, just take the top half"
>
> **Big Man**: "Okaaaaay. If you say so. "

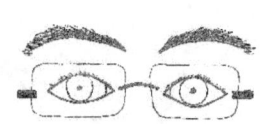

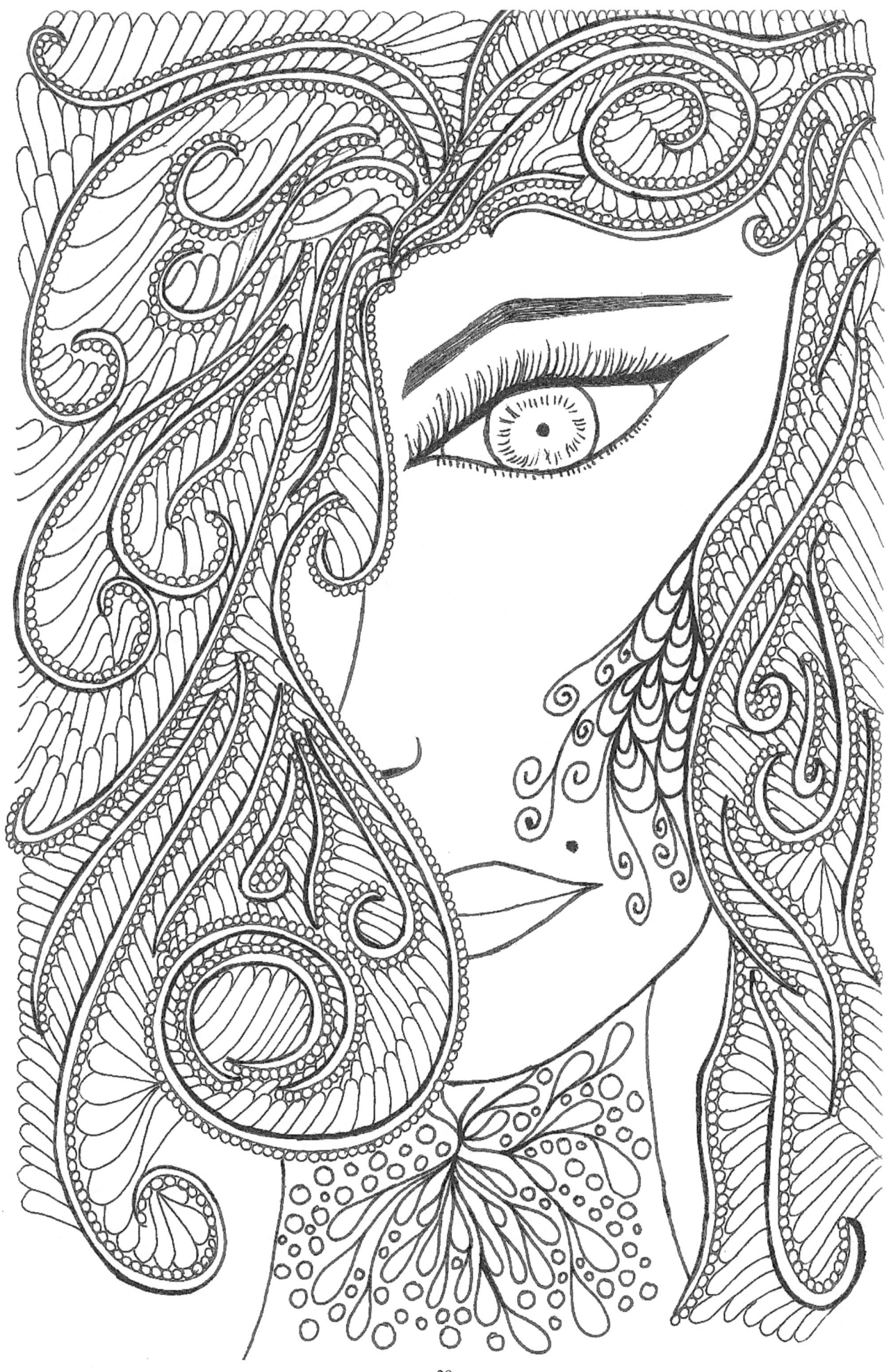

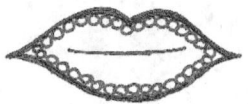

Neighbour staring out of the window: "Errrrr Rash? What are you doing mate?"

Rash: "You know! Just taking my profile photo to make myself look nicer and a bit older. Needed a bush!!!!"

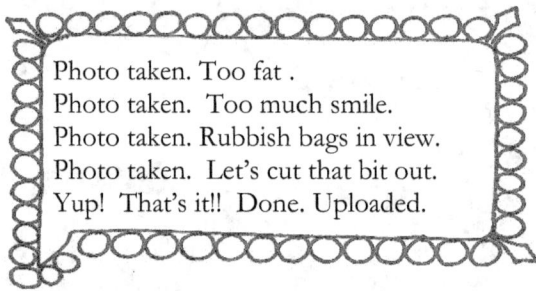

Photo taken. Too fat .
Photo taken. Too much smile.
Photo taken. Rubbish bags in view.
Photo taken. Let's cut that bit out.
Yup! That's it!! Done. Uploaded.

The whole escapade was ridiculous. Literally ridiculous. What are we really trying to achieve when doing these silly things? To get that one photo, I had debated with my husband, sounded like an idiot, made myself look like a plonker standing in the middle of rubbish bags, and then got caught by my neighbour!! How shameful.

I am the worst at natural poses and I hate being caught out by a camera. I take so many photos but crop out the crap all the time. This is one of the biggest reasons I feel that what we share may not be all it seems. My own behaviour should tell me that if I am doing it, then so are others so stop believing all you see.

In fairness to my friends though, a lot of effort went into that photo as you can tell, so thank you to all those who liked it!

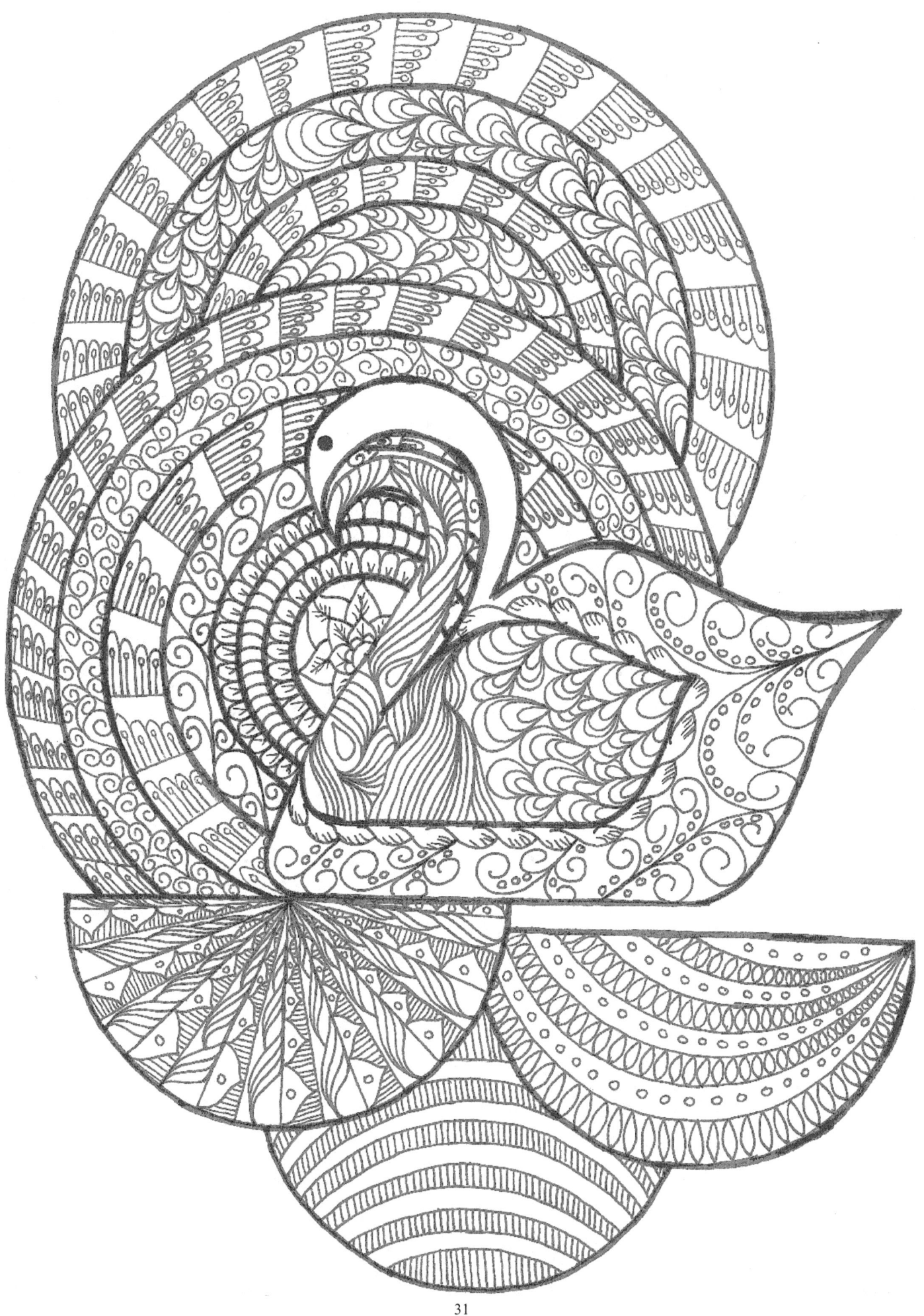

PANDA

I did this doodle one day while my husband was on a work trip in China and it got me thinking of course.

Doesn't it sound so cool? Working abroad. People check in on social media and everyone sees it. So and so is at Heathrow Terminal 5 (just so you know they are flying British Airways of course) with the strap line "Work". "Ohhhh look at me while everyone else is off to some office or factory. My work is so important that I have an impact on another country!" Well bully for you.

Now the flip side. Having been in both situations I can say that in my experience the partner left at home is like a single parent struggling to sort kids, work, house and madness. The person abroad is on a schedule. Hotel, conference room, office. Hotel, conference room, office. Then flight home. Most evenings are nice though. A few beers and a nice meal but all the while watching every word that comes out of your mouth as you need to be careful with your boss or your client etc.

And of course what we cannot forget is the rocking partner sat on the stairs waiting for the other one to come home and take over. It doesn't matter if they've had a fourteen hour flight home and haven't slept. It's their turn!!

Children are very tolerant and don't even notice it most of the time but I do remember one time my daughter cried her eyes out when I told her I was going for two nights. It broke my heart. Suddenly hubby walked in to two ladies crying and he casually said "Sweetheart do you want cheese and beans jacket potato for dinner tomorrow?" All crying stopped. Like, literally just stopped. I learned a big lesson that day. When one of us goes away, nobody is to dwell on it. We all just get on with it and time passes far quicker.

And then off course comes the sneaky judgement from people. "Have you ever noticed how he is always working away from home? I wonder if he's sneaking around with another woman"
Or
"She's always away with work, that poor husband of hers has to do everything". Do you see the difference?

But the honest truth is that work is work. It's something to post about and a nice change to the everyday routine. So what if my husband goes to China and has a nice meal in the evening? Good on him!! And so what if someone tells you they are away from home. Maybe it's their lovely way of saying "I'm away, please look after my partner".

Personally I enjoy seeing posts like this. I love seeing my friends doing well in their careers and it spurs me on even further. But I'm aware not everyone is quite so proud of their friends.

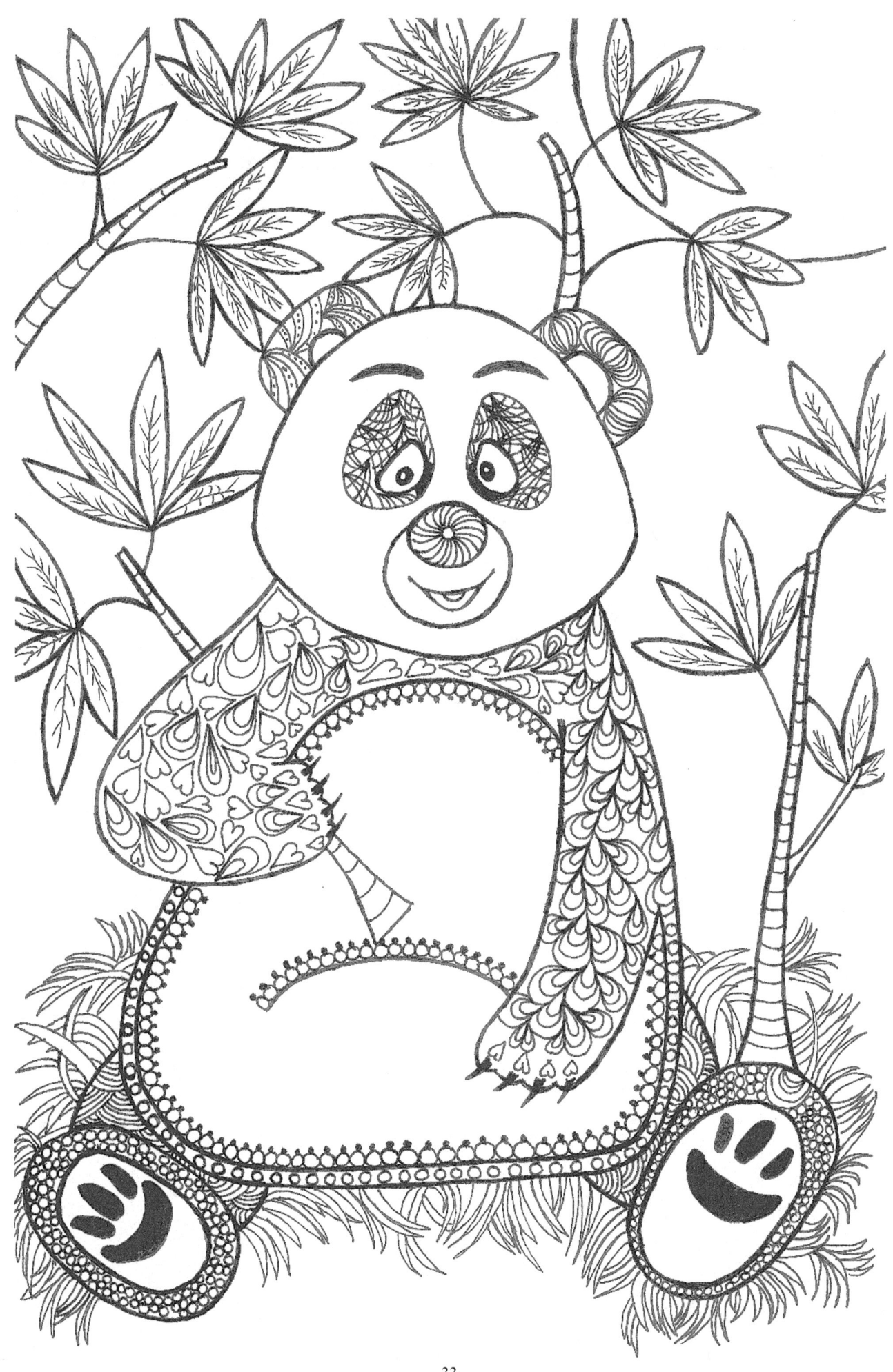

DREAM CATCHER

I wonder how many people dream of the day they are a social media superstar?

What an aim. To be someone who craves the attention of a bunch of strangers. This makes me want to laugh and cry at the same time. The number of profiles I see of young people that have opened up their lives to the public has increased year on year and I don't believe it's good for mental health.   A long term study conducted in the Nordics followed 20,000 people who had just joined in with the social media world. As you can imagine, statistically, many of them were younger as they had just been given parental permission to use social media. Within the first 12-18 months, reports of anxiety and depression dramatically increased but then fell to a normal rate after this period of time. As a possible conclusion to the study, this may show that the first few months of using social media are delicate and if we can understand it for what it really is and see past the nastiness, then in the long run, you should be ok.

However, looking at the comments on some of the posts, I see the nastiest, evil, ill-educated comments one could see. It seems there are many out there who love to bring people down. A recent documentary about trolling was aired, showing the effects it had on the Jesy Nelson as a young woman in the spotlight. Now Jesy Nelson was a young lady who wanted to sing and was thrown into the air of fame on the X-Factor, but there are many young people who are choosing this as their careers. An internet star is now a career but they seem to avoid the reality of what they will have to face and the comments they will endure.

On the flip side to this, have you seen the crap they post?! Blimey. It's all quite attention seeking really. But why do they want this exposure and attention? Why would anyone want to do this to themselves?

How has it even become possible that young people dream of such careers? A life of saying stupid things and posting photos of trashy rubbish.

I'm never going to understand this dream.

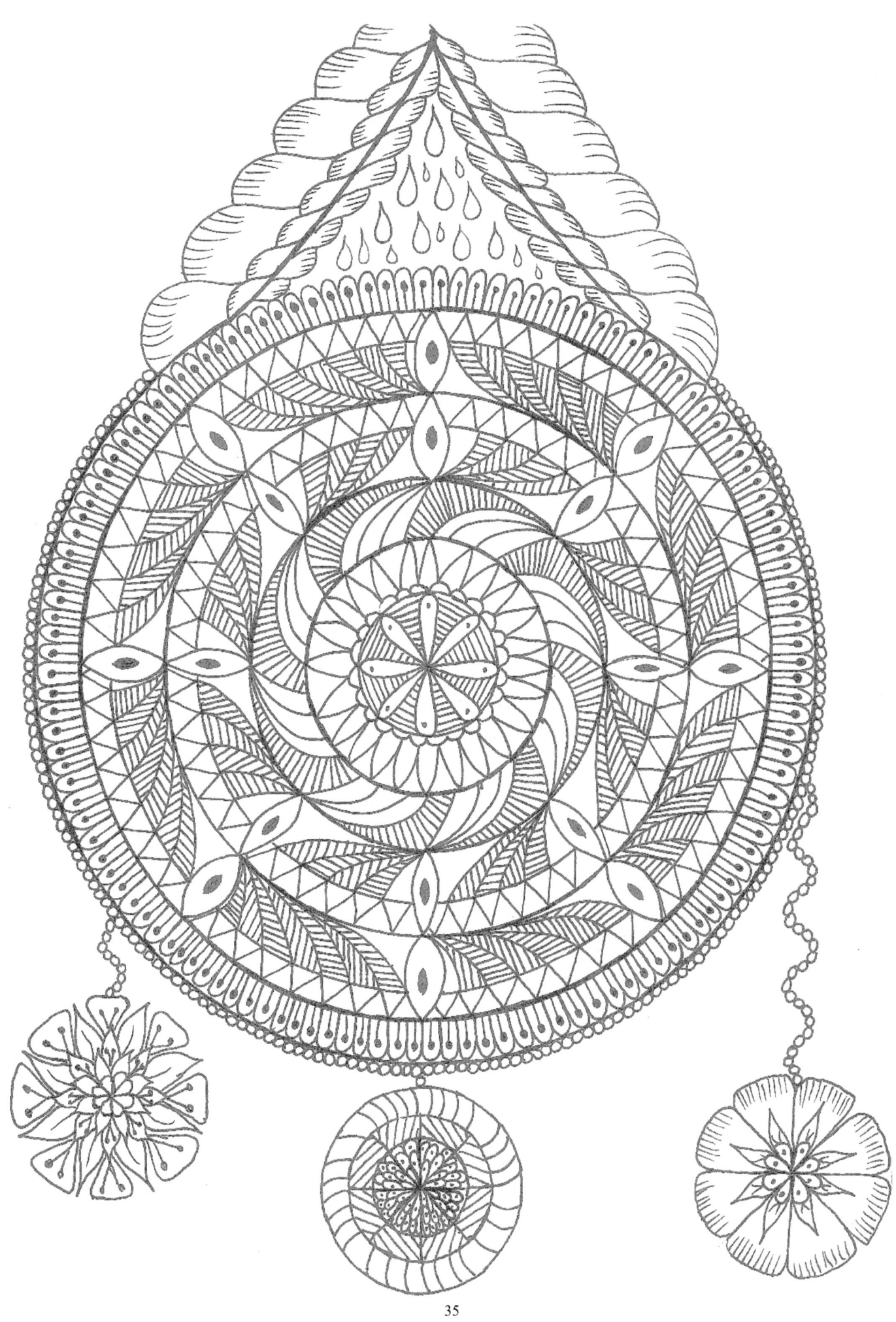

PLATE GATE

One winter, two friends and I met up for a bite to eat, a good old natter and catch up. The photo looked so civilized. We looked like three professional women in our work clothes who had met after work for a lovely evening out. One could easily be mistaken to think we spoke about intelligent things like careers and leadership, or even our latest projects and work issues.

The reality was simple. That week all three of us felt like we had been dragged through a hedge backwards but one particular friend was contending with something far more serious. This was a three month visit from the father-in-law who lives in the US but retirement brought long visits.

Not only had the visit exhausted her, she proceeded to explain that her father-in-law had made the decision he didn't like her crockery and took it upon himself to not only buy a new set but come back to the house, pack up her old set and replace it with the hideous one he had bought!!!

Now this in itself was not the worst crime but after two months of being judged by the father-in-law for being a working mother, the plate replacement was just the straw that broke the camel's back for her to completely flip! To the other friend and myself, it was funny but for the friend who had to deal with the situation, it was super annoying. Poor lady was exhausted, fed up and very angry.

Suffice to say she was brilliant and told her father-in-law to get her pristine white crockery back, pack up his hideous plates in the cupboard and return them to the shop. Drama over but anger had remained for an extra few days.

On the upside, the story got labelled "plate gate", which meant we always had a reference point in time.
Next time you see a photo of your girlfriends out having a lovely meal, just remember that they probably spent the whole night moaning.

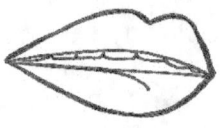
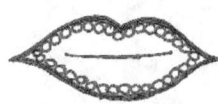

"….he never helps around the house"
"…I'm sick of my life!!"
"…..did you see what that w****r did?!"
"…...I'm broke"

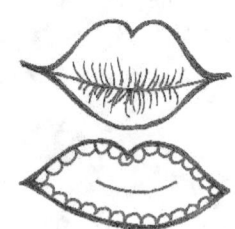

When you look at it this way, why would you feel jealous of that?

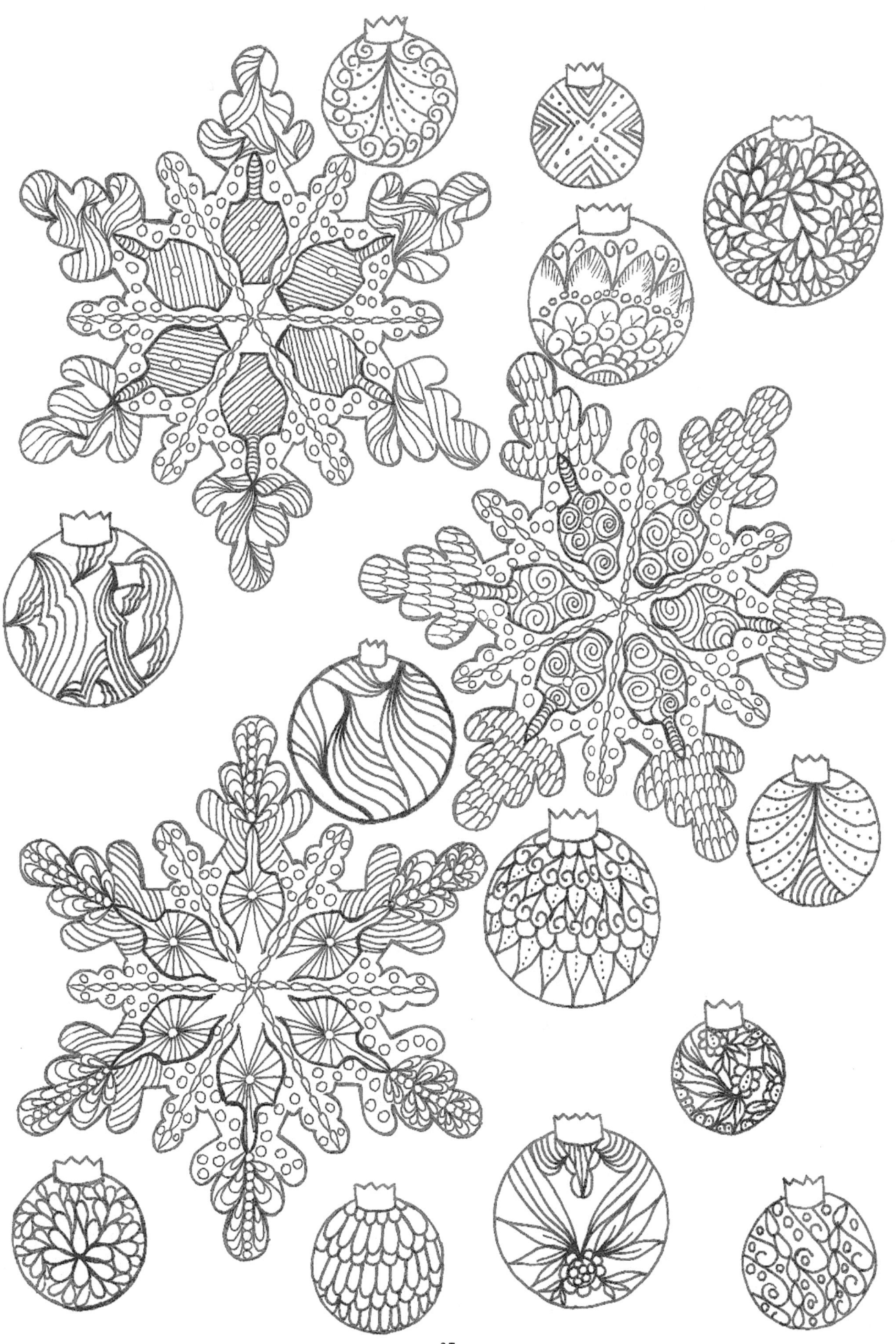

RELIGION

I like to class myself as a semi practicing Hindu. I'm unsure of whether there is a god or not, but just in case there is, I will continue to practice all the religious events which involve eating sweets. There comes a time where you have to sacrifice for the greater good, and if eating Indian sweets helps this, then I shall partake. And of course when the school asks me to pop in and help educate the children on Hinduism, I will begin the process of learning on Google to make myself sound knowledgeable.

However, all joking aside, there are countless connections I have who do practice their religion and enjoy sharing their experiences on social media and a majority of these posts are very welcomed by the community. Seeing my friends have such strong faith makes me happy and in some ways helps me to know that they are being guided by a higher purpose. Religion gives people support, love and a community in troubled times and this is a truly special thing.

So where's the issue? When religious belief cross into political territories, this causes conflict. Very recently, a friend of mine who is a devout Christian posted an article about abortion, as they are against it due to religious belief. There was an immediate backlash here and the opinion conflicted with many people regarding their right to choose what happens with their bodies. Oddly, this happened with another friend of mine on the same subject fairly recently but at least people were a little politer on that post. I think my response was a bit direct though.

Not long before this, an Islamic friend of mine posted a quote from the Quran with his interpretation regarding why war has to happen. Again, significant backlash from his colleagues and friends as one can imagine.

Stock summary

Religion = lovely

Political subjects = mmmmm

Religion + political subjects = proceed with great caution

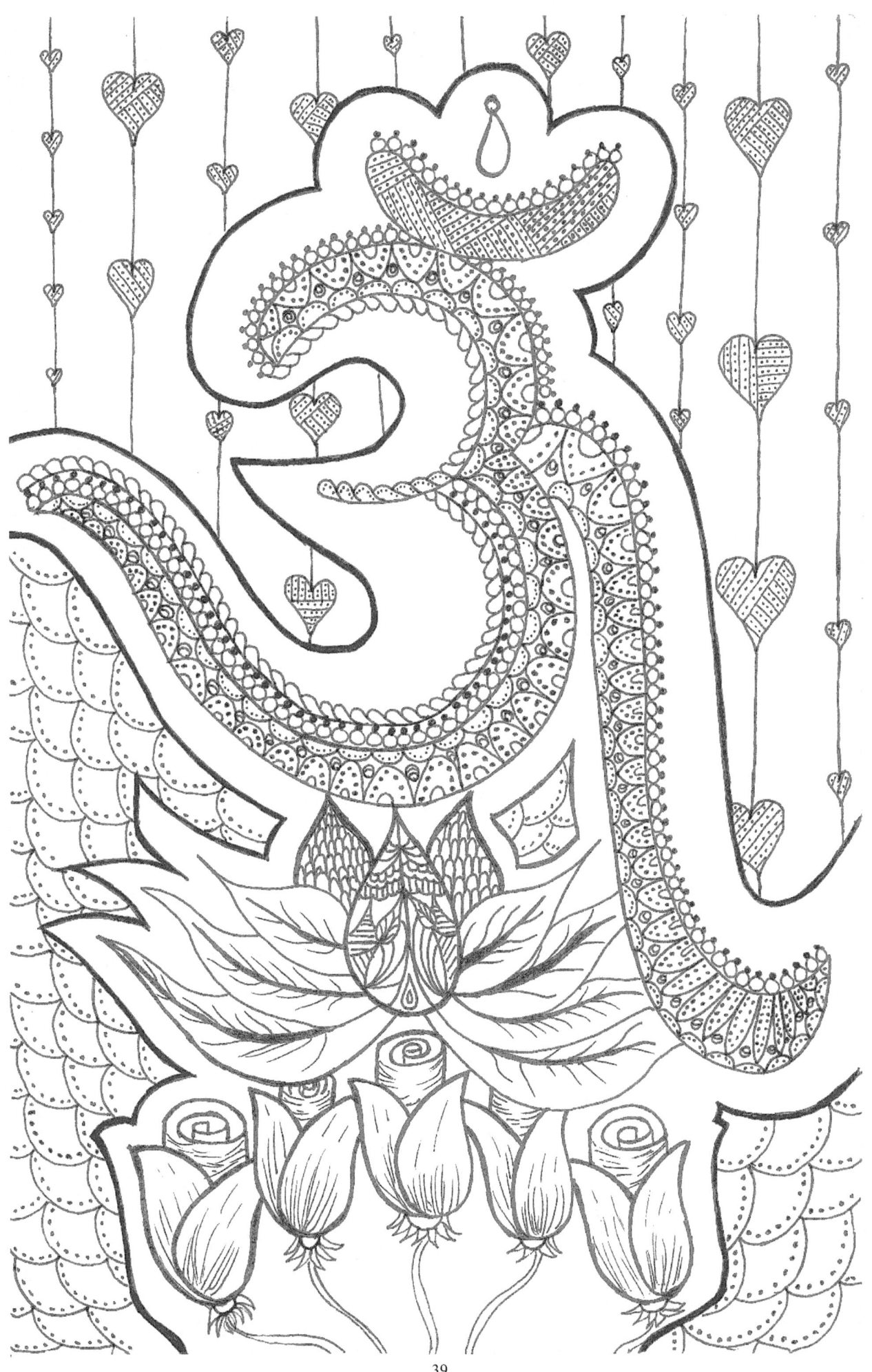

MY DAUGHTER AND I

There is a photo of my daughter and I. It received many comments and likes. At the time we were on holiday in Malta and my husband was watching her and I talking, and took a picture. It is a photo of love. Pure love. I think she was talking about how her friends at school would love to wear a skirt like hers and do ballet. Her little dreams seemed so important and I just had to listen to everything. School gossip is top notch stuff if you listen closely.

There are real moments when social media is a true reflection of the photo itself. To me, that was a perfect day, a perfect moment and my daughter is the perfect kid (at the moment anyway).

When my husband posted it, I think he wanted the world to see how proud he was of his "little ladies" and it was real. Not fake or posed but this made me realize that people like my husband only post real things.

Instead of looking at posts and wondering if they are real, it may be worth thinking about the person who did the posting. Are they a genuine character who is not after attention? If the answer is yes, then the likelihood is that their social media will be truthful and authentic.

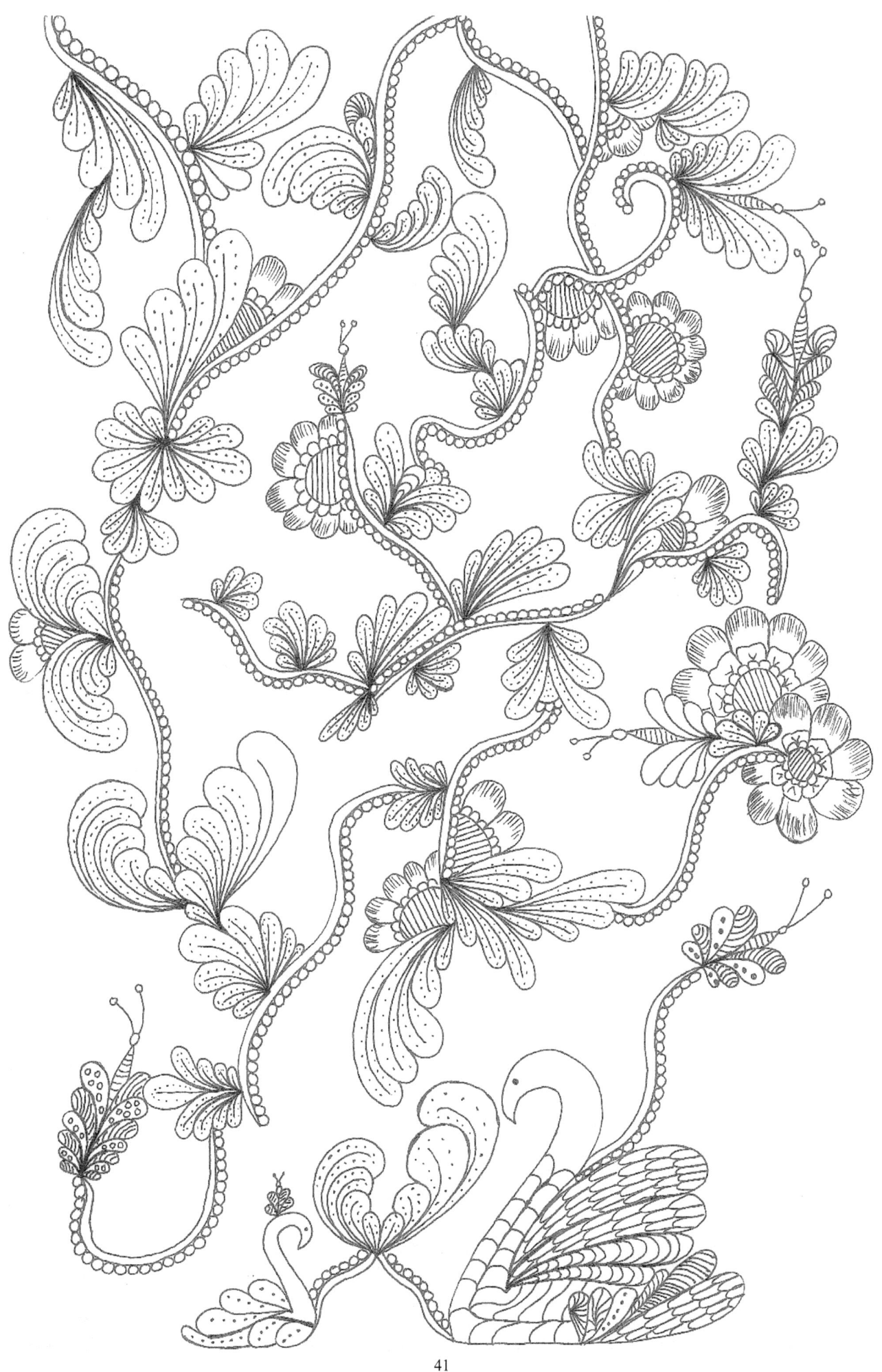

SHARE, SHARE, SHARE

Recently I saw a share about a missing girl. It was awful. A beautiful girl went missing in Birmingham at a party and the family have been looking for her.

However, when looking into it further, I realized that the post was from about six months ago and was in Birmingham, Pennsylvania in the USA. Sadly, the young three year old was found dead three months later and so the post was irrelevant, in the wrong country and just all round sad and awful.

A year ago I was with a lovely colleague on my team and she told me that her previous manager had asked her to think about removing a post about foxes from her timeline as she worked in the pharmaceutical industry and the source of the post was PETA. Whoops. All my colleague wanted to do was share a post about a sad fox. Poor lady.

Now for my own. About three years ago I shared a post showing my respect for an elderly gentleman who had fought in the war. It received many likes but suddenly a comment came through asking me:

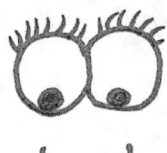   "Rash I didn't know you supported the BNP".

I don't. Let me be clear but it turned out the source of the photo was one from the British National Party site!! I didn't even once check it. I removed it very quickly as I don't wish to be associated with anything political but subsequent to that moment, I now check every share to look for the date, the source and the country.

We've all seen the posts:
Dog missing - article created in 2018
Latest article on poo on the McDonalds screens - originally posted in 2016 and therefore nothing new. They haven't gone down the pan as a result so no one cared.
A scare article on how livestock are treated - article originated in Outer Mongolia and totally irrelevant in the UK.

You get my drift here. So when you next see an article which throws you sideways, before you get your ninja fast fingers out to work and share it, just take a quick scan through to see where it came from. It will definitely save you some time deleting it or justifying it later.

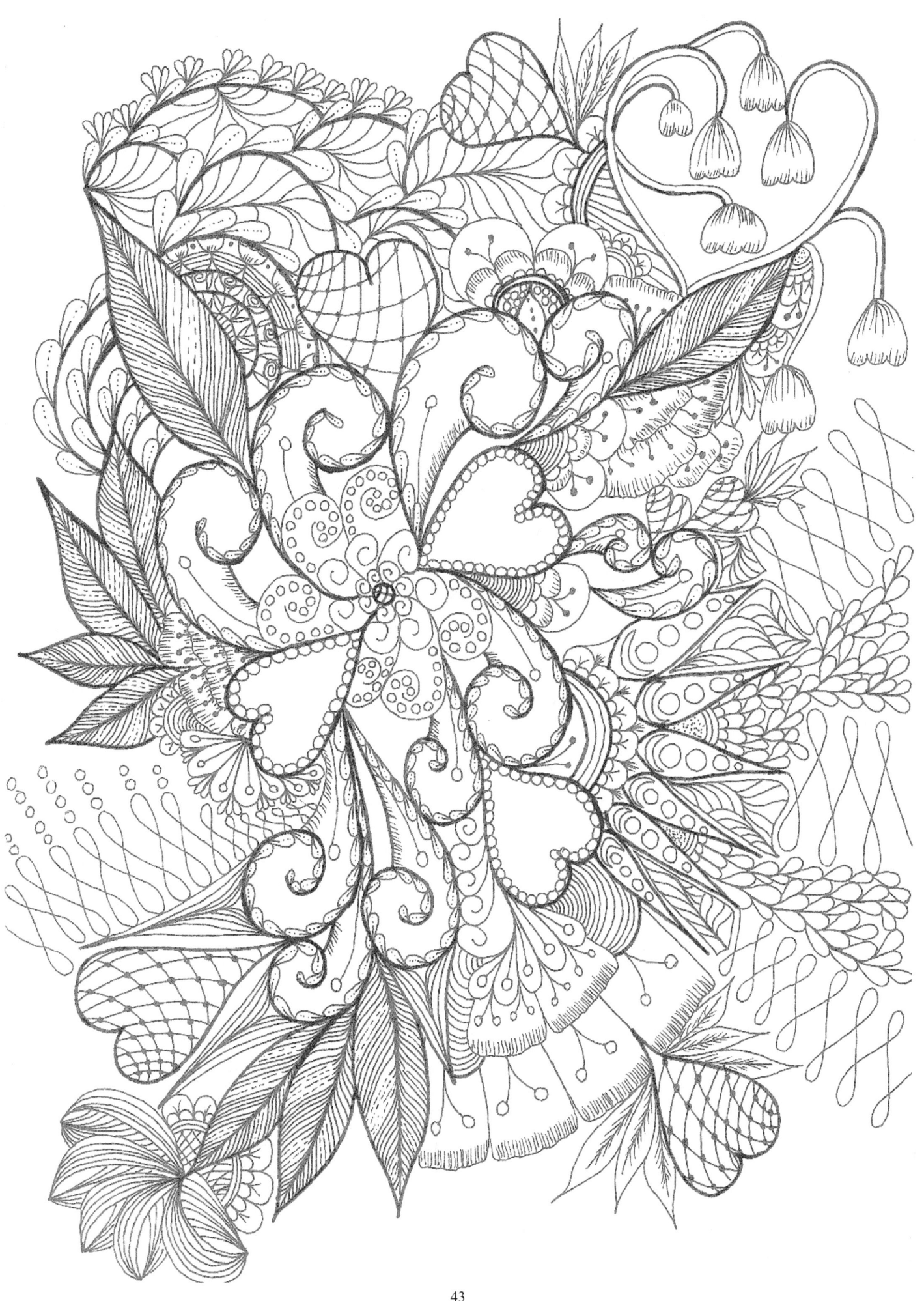

BEAUTIFUL

The word beautiful is such an elegant one. It's positive, kind and up-lifting.
Personally, I love using this word. Those who know me, know I use it freely with genuine meaning and care.

"You look beautiful!"
"That's a beautiful photo of you"
"Oh my god, you look beautiful in that dress."

Other alternative words are available but you get my train of thought, however generally speaking I don't think we use it enough when our friends post photos.

We are very good at the "reduced value" comment.

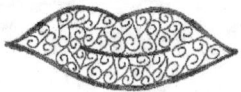
"Love that dress. Can I buy it when you're finished with it?"
"Looks like a nice evening."
"Oh that's a great venue. Loved it when I was last there. "

Why do we do this? Why can't we freely say that someone looks superb?! What's wrong with us? If someone has made an effort then surely they should be rewarded with a genuinely nice compliment. It doesn't hurt us. It doesn't demean us and it certainly helps the other person.

And if they look like trash just don't say anything. Back to the silence page.

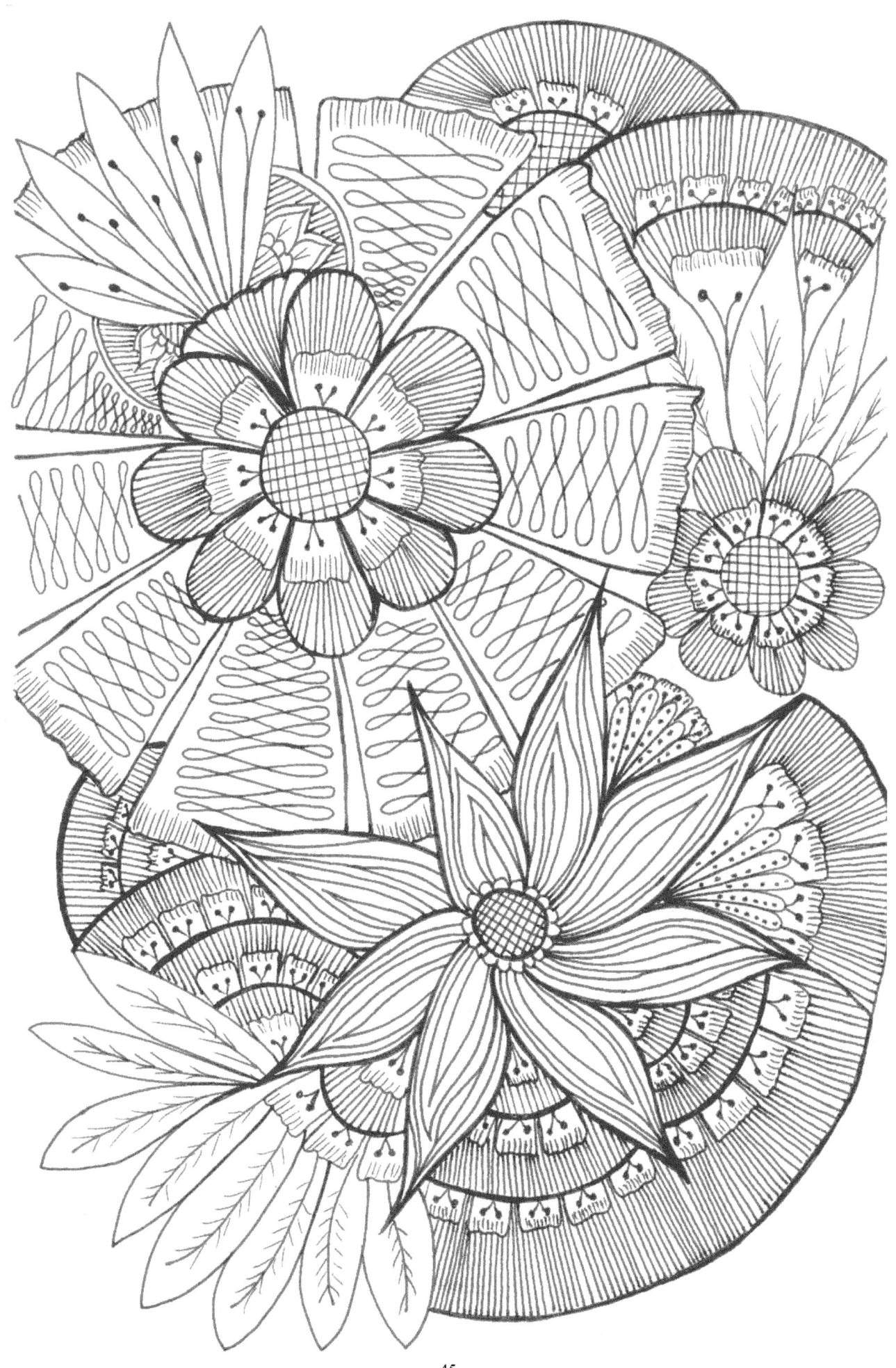

CHANGE OF SEASONS

Whether the sun is out or the leaves are falling in autumn, one post I love to see is the great British weather moan. They make my day.

In a world where we are debating, clicking, sharing, bitching or praising, the one area we seem to be united about is the weather. Now I am a cold person, so when someone posts they are turning the heating on, I feel this overwhelming sense of relief. In that moment there is officially someone else in my little community.

It is even the moment I am allowed to wear fluffy bed socks and fur lined pyjamas. I don't see an issue with this but I'm sure it's not my husband's cuppa if you know what I mean. And then of course there is the opposite.

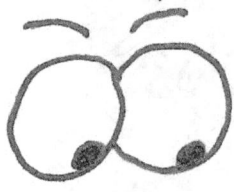
"It's too hot!!"
"I can't sleep"
"Is it just me or have the spiders started seeking revenge?"
"I'm sick of this rain"
"Check in at the hospital with no explanation looking for attention"
> "You ok babes?"
> "What's happened? Everything ok?"

Then of course one hundred comments later you see this person has slipped on the falling leaves and broken an ankle. Whoops.

We love to moan about it. But in fairness it unites us all. In fact, I would go as far to say that the British weather makes me proud. I would hate to live in a country where the climate is the same all year round. It would just be boring. Clothes styles would stay the same, the food we eat would not be seasonal and everyone would be broke if we spent every night chilling in the local beer garden.

Roll on the next season and roll on the great British moaning.

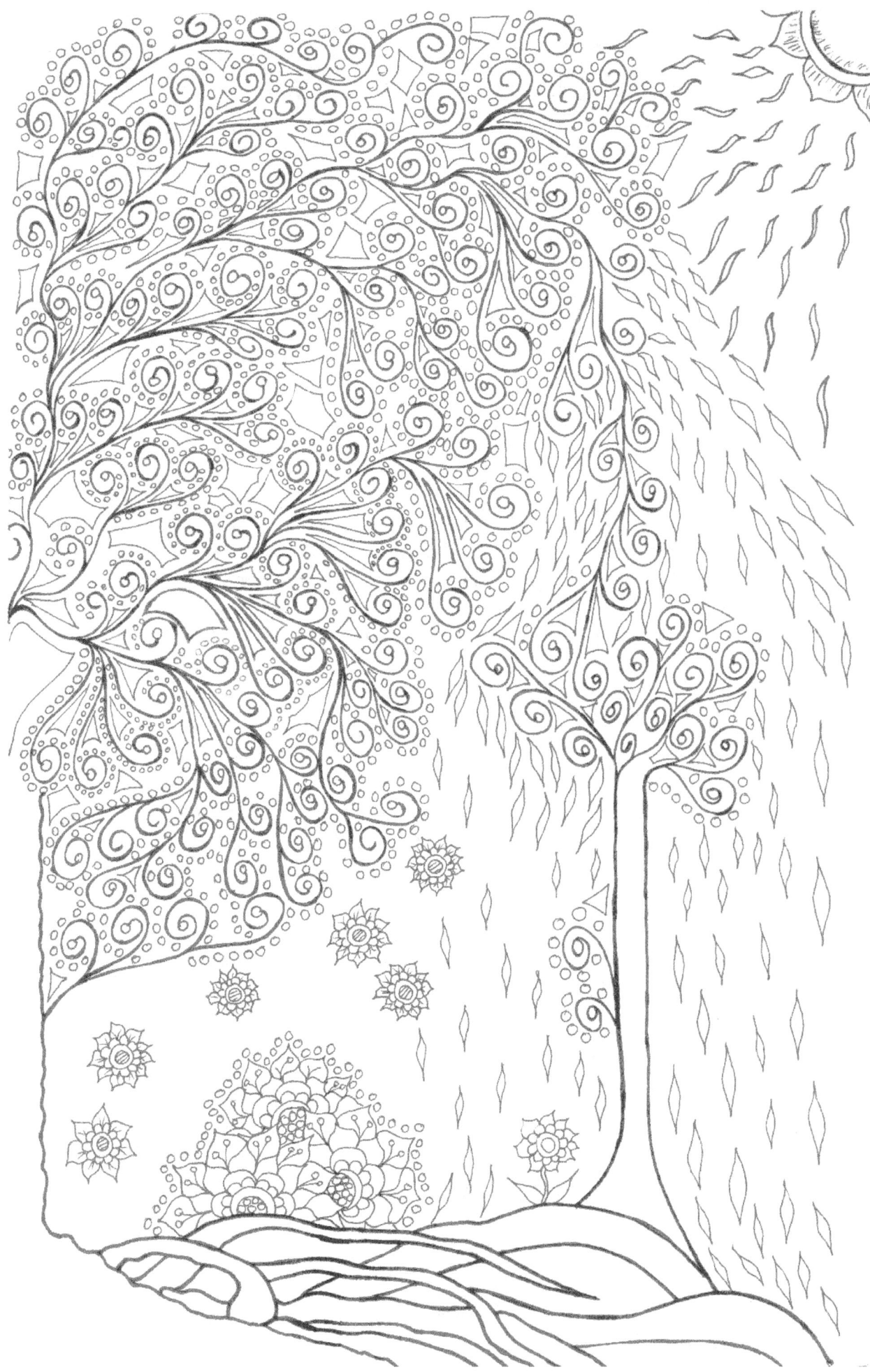

FAMILY HOLIDAY

"322 days to go!! We're booked! We're off to Spain! Holibobs! I'm on my way. Woooo hoooo!"

Airport check in post. Tick
Glass of wine in lounge post. Tick
Random ugly feet on a beach post. Tick
Living my best life post. Tick

REALITY

Rash: "Your holiday looked incredible!"
Friends: "Rash you have no idea. My kids were complete shits and we didn't sleep one night"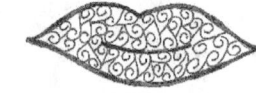

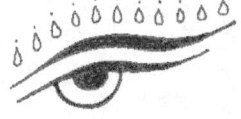 **Rash**: "Looked like you had a lovely time on holiday. The kids looked so happy!"
Friend: I spent the whole holiday trying to control my boys temper. One day he threw the biggest strop and it was so embarrassing. I hated it. I'm never going with my kids again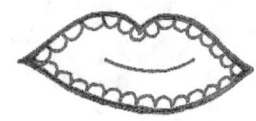

Rash: I'm so pleased you got some time with your family over the holidays. You work so hard and you really deserve it.
Friend: My daughters fought every, single, day. I couldn't wait to go back to work. Holidays are overrated and they did my head in!!! And to top it off my husband did my head in. How am I going to retire with him?!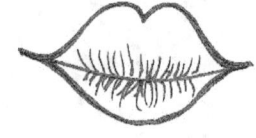

As hard as some holidays can be, we never post the bad bits. We show the world how fabulous our kids are, how hot the weather is or how relaxed we are, when in reality this may not be true. But I have never understood why we do this, because essentially we are lying and making some of our friends jealous of our holidays, and yet if they knew the reality, this wouldn't be the case!

On a serious note I have recently done some research on this topic and have just come to learn that the financial Ombudsman have released some guidance on holidays and social media. Did you know that you could actually be invalidating your home insurance by posting that you are away? Some companies even have guidelines on the number of "friends" you have. If this is over 450 then they will not guarantee a pay-out if your house is robbed in your absence as they will question your relationship with that many people. Now in fairness to the insurance company here, it does clearly state in most policies that your absences should not be advertised, and posting on social media will do exactly that. Something to think about.

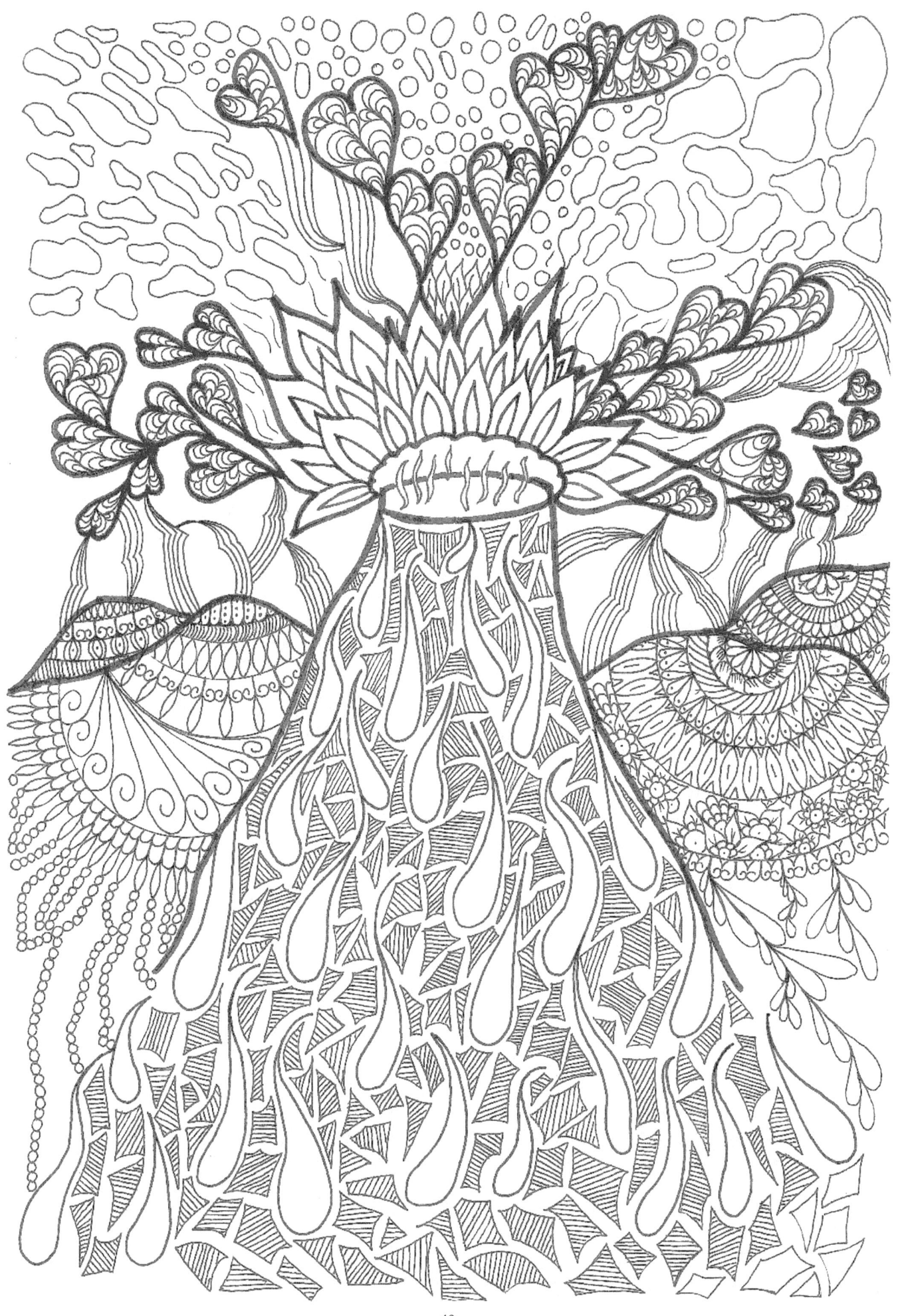

2018 SWAN

Photos on social media are a snapshot moment of someone's life. It represents a single moment at a time but yet there are many hours across the day that are not represented.

In 2018, I actively posted on Facebook around 115 times. I was tagged by other people too which added to this but from myself on Facebook, it was about 115 times. On average this is just over twice a week. Most posts were about family celebrations, dogs, cats and some other random bits but nothing nasty about anyone or any rants. I never post about political issues or say awful things so all in, pretty clean going on Facebook.

However, to everyone else, life looked good but behind the scenes there was an awful lot happening in my world. The twice a week posts were those small moments in my life where something nice happened and I wanted to share it because most of the time I was just exhausted.

I had taken on a new role at work, then a restructure happened, my husband had an operation, my son wasn't very well and I took on a whole new team and had to embed myself in a new structure with a new manager. I was tired. I can promise you this was just the tip of what was happening.

On New Year's Eve I did this doodle as I couldn't wait for the year to end and I desperately wanted to start again. Just remember, when you see something on social media that makes you jealous, just remember, this is one single moment. You haven't seen the rest of the week. It's not always rosey.

I'm not saying people are lying but I think people are reaching out to show something nice. Even if it is a single moment. Be nice and hit the like button. It won't hurt you. I promise.

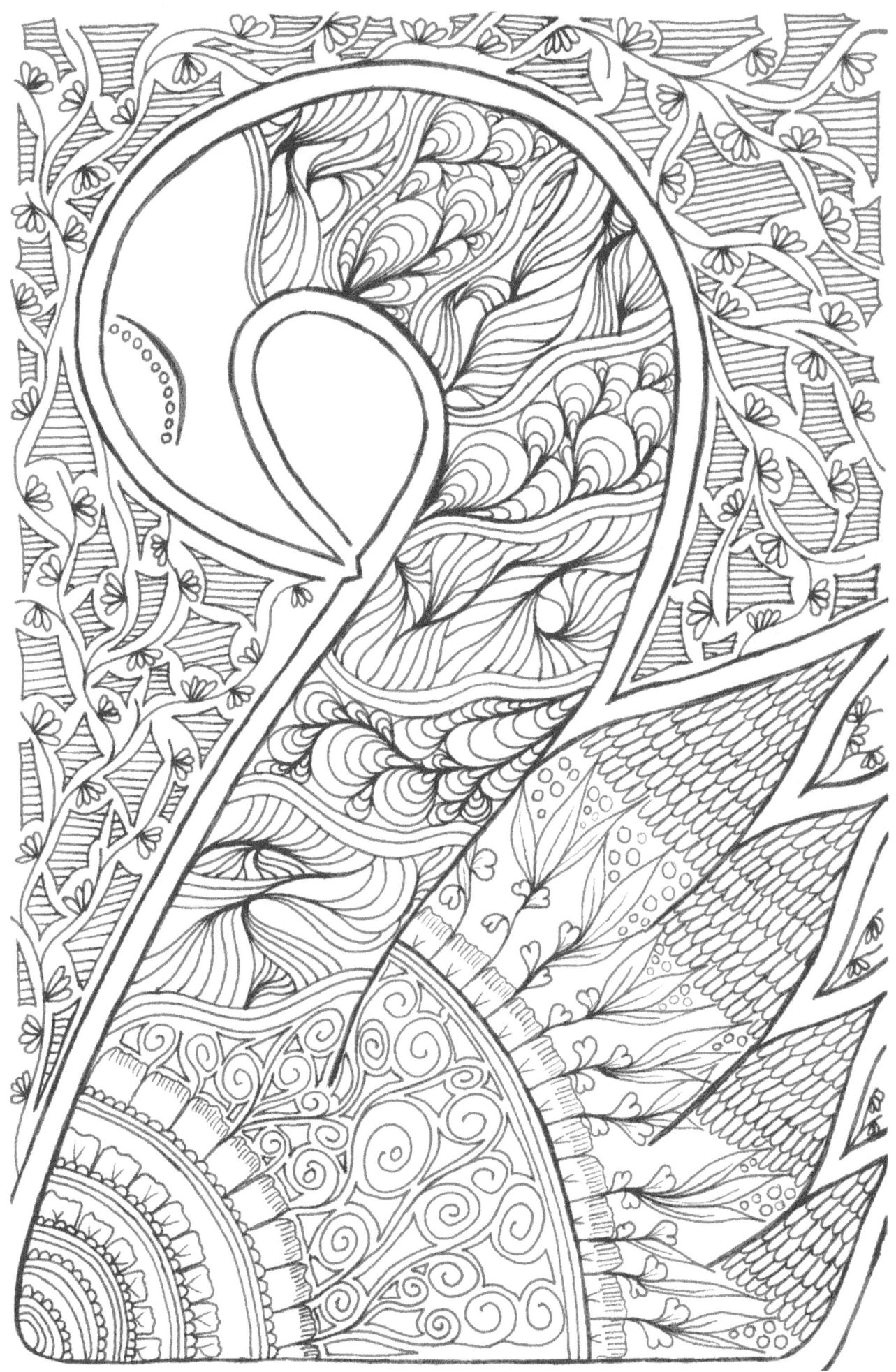

VAGUE POSTS

Now come on!! You immediately know what I'm talking about here. You've seen those posts. You've got irritated at those posts and you've chosen to ignore them or you have done it. You've replied:

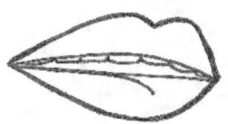

"You ok babes?"
"Everything ok?"
"O.M.G what's happened?"

The best response of all:

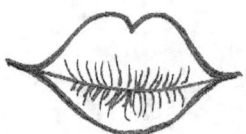

"Will inbox you babes"

My opinion is clear on this. In any given day there is a crisis in almost everyone's world and in that moment you will call about two friends or family members to have a good old rant and tell them what's happening. Lovely.

But then you will do something stupid and post on social media:

Joe Bloggs is fed up
Susan Smith is feeling lost
Chris Clay is feeling sore at the hospital

Random posts with no explanation. So you have phoned two people but you have 300 friends on Facebook. You haven't called all three hundred to explain what is going on so 298 have no idea. I will almost guarantee that about 200 of your left out friends will think you are attention seeking, 50 won't even look and the remaining 48 probably just want the gossip and ask you if you are ok.

I'm totally baffled by these posts. Just say what's happening or don't post. Please save us all.

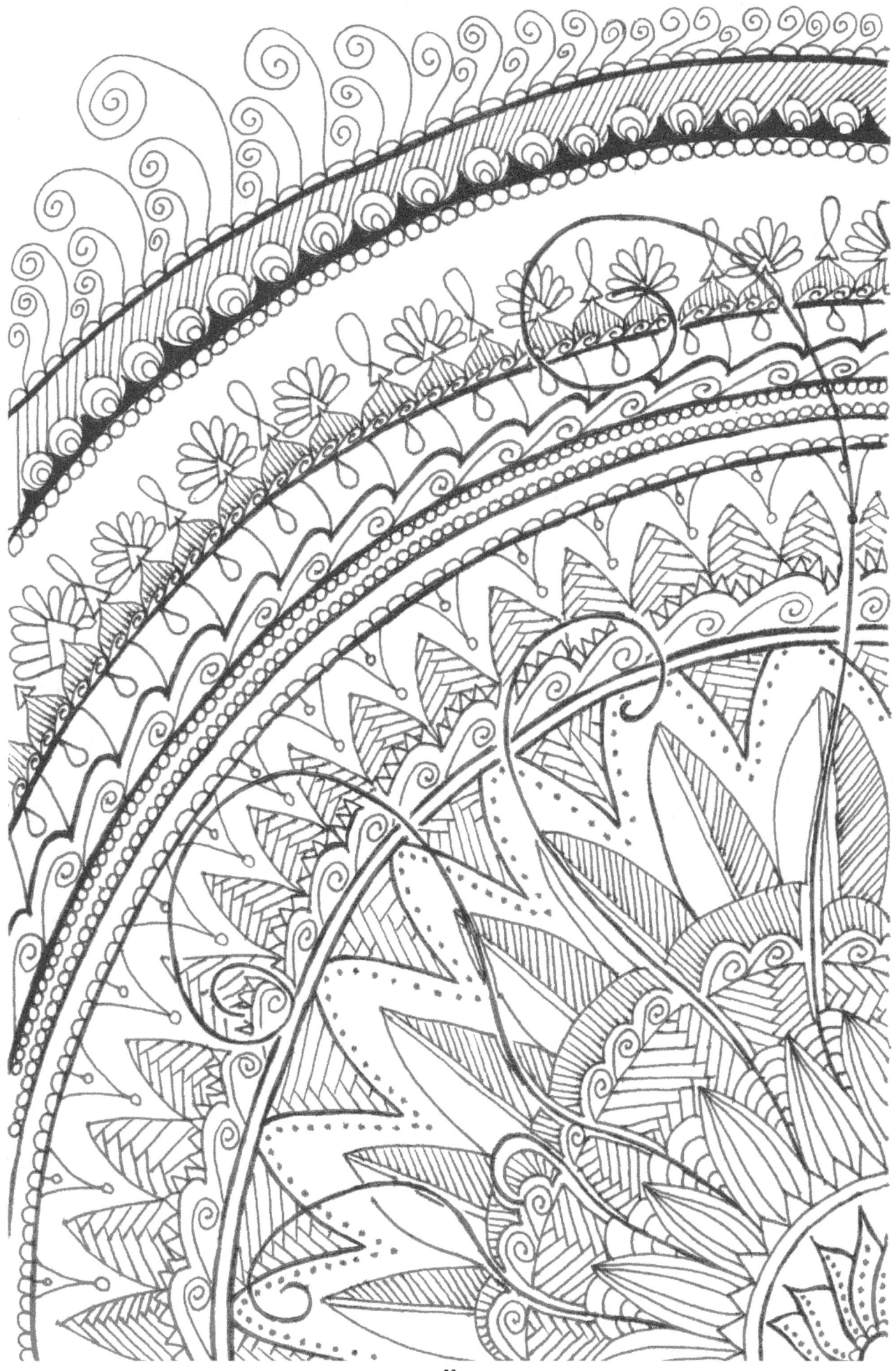

GRIEF

I was 22 when I met the Big Man. A year after we met, we bought our first house but culturally it was not acceptable for us to live together prior to marriage. We followed the rules and hubby lived in our home and I lived happily with Mum and Dad, knowing I had my home to go to when we married a year later.

I didn't want my man to be on his own, even though he was quite happy, so off I trotted to the RSPCA and brought back two kittens who were brother and sister. I have no idea how they got called Max and Shirley but that's what happened. Seventeen years later, our Shirley fell ill and got old and we had to let her go over the "Rainbow Bridge", as people have lovingly termed it.

When I posted about this, it got my thinking about why we share stories of grief with the world and in that moment, I wanted to let people know that my world had significantly changed when the cat died. I suppose I also wanted everyone to know that I wasn't in the mood to answer the phone or reply to messages. After all, our animals are the children who never stop relying on us, and so it felt very heart breaking to say goodbye.

When people post about their losses, some say little and others post weekly or daily. I'm not sure why but some have said it makes them feel connected to the deceased, while others are reaching out to their friends and asking for help. I don't think there is any right or wrong on this subject. I simply hope it gives them the comfort they need. My only real thought here is that if one doesn't get that comfort from social media, they may want to consider alternative methods like grief counselling.

Oddly enough, I tried this doodle concept twice before this one was created and this was started one hour after finding out my husband's grandfather had passed away. I was just quietly saddened when suddenly the other two attempts didn't seem good enough, but there is an error in this. I'm sure you will spot it but I simply didn't have the heart to remove it. Grief can be very painful for people and sometimes when it happens, we make little errors. I'm happy to admit it.

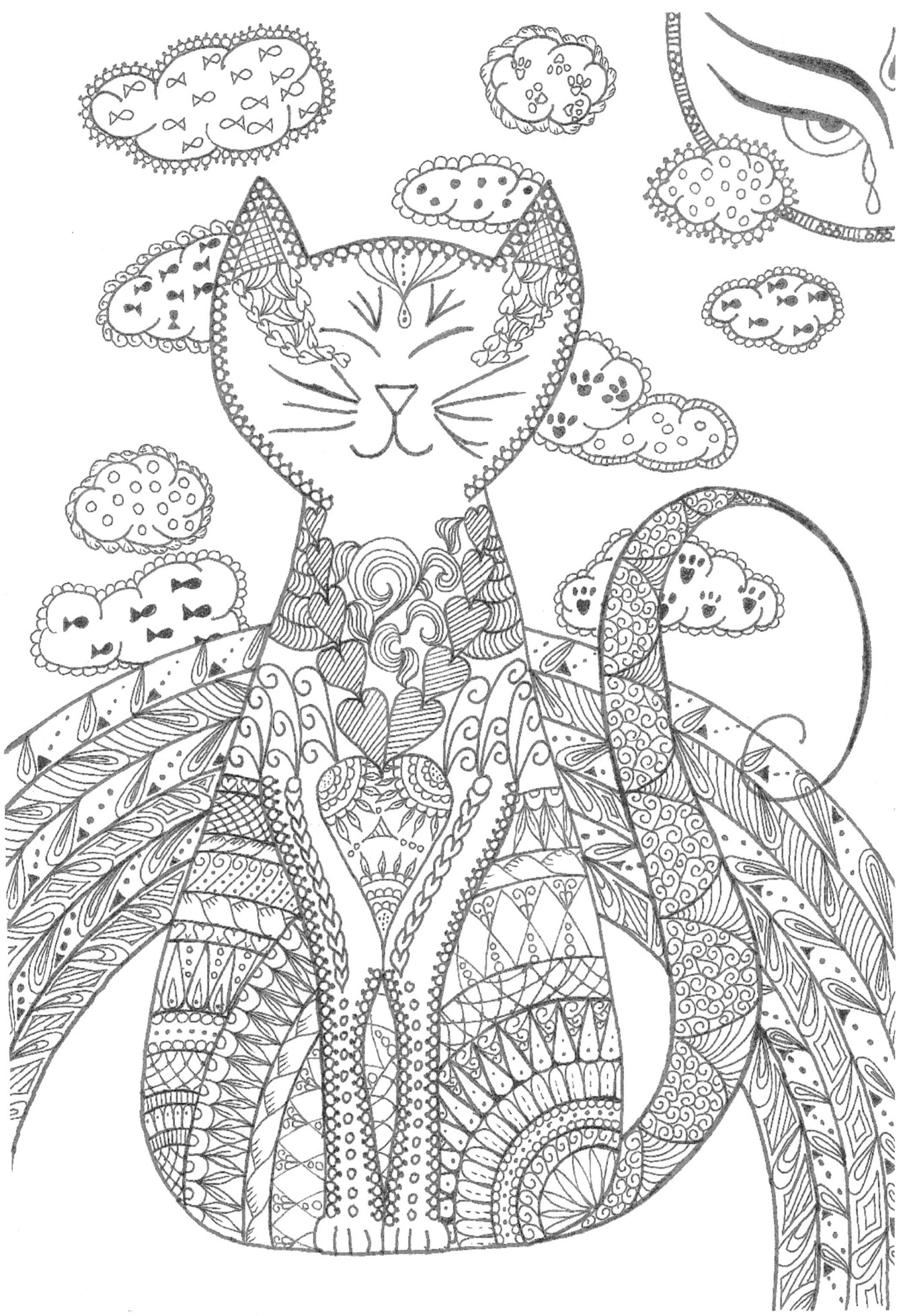

PLEB

One of my closest friends Sarah emigrated to Australia two years ago and I remember feeling incredibly sad when she left. I had worked with her for over ten years and she decided to be selfless and support her husband in his next career move abroad. Time went by and two years passed, when one day she announced need she was visiting the UK and would like to meet up with the old team we worked on.

Obviously, I jumped at the chance of this as I was so excited to see her and the others. In fact that day, I must have been so excited that I completely missed all the messages with the correct time and was over an hour early. So this obviously means I have to doodle and look like an interesting person in some random hotel bar.

I realized in that moment that doodling stops me from feeling like a pleb but most people use social media for this job. God forbid we walk into a hotel, restaurant or anywhere and sit down on our own and just people watch. So instead what do we do? We get out our phones and try and look like we have lots of friends or make out that we aren't on our own for long as we think we look like plebs.

I see this all the time. People sat on their phones on Facebook, Instagram, Snap Chat or whatever it might be just so they don't have to look up as they think everyone will be staring at them because they are on their own. How dare they be?!

The best one though has got to be the two minute call. You know your friend will be there soon. She or he has never been late before. So instead of just waiting you get out your phone and make a call to a random person you haven't caught up with and suddenly now you look like an important pleb because you're on the phone. As predicted, your friend has now walked through the door and you have to end the call with your other pal so you make some excuse to get them off the phone. At this point, you have now pointlessly made a call which you couldn't continue, all in the name of not wanting to sit on your own for two minutes.

Most excuses I've heard include:

"Oh no! I can't believe this call is now coming in. I really need to take this I'm so sorry"
"Dammit I've called you and just got the battery beep. Can I call you later?"
"Shit! Mum's on the other line. Gotta go hun"

It's all such a waste of time. Try carrying a good book, a doodle pad, a crossword or why not just consider sitting there looking like a pleb for five minutes? People watching is far more interesting than social media.

However, any more than five minutes, get the phone out and back on social media. People might think you're a pervert.

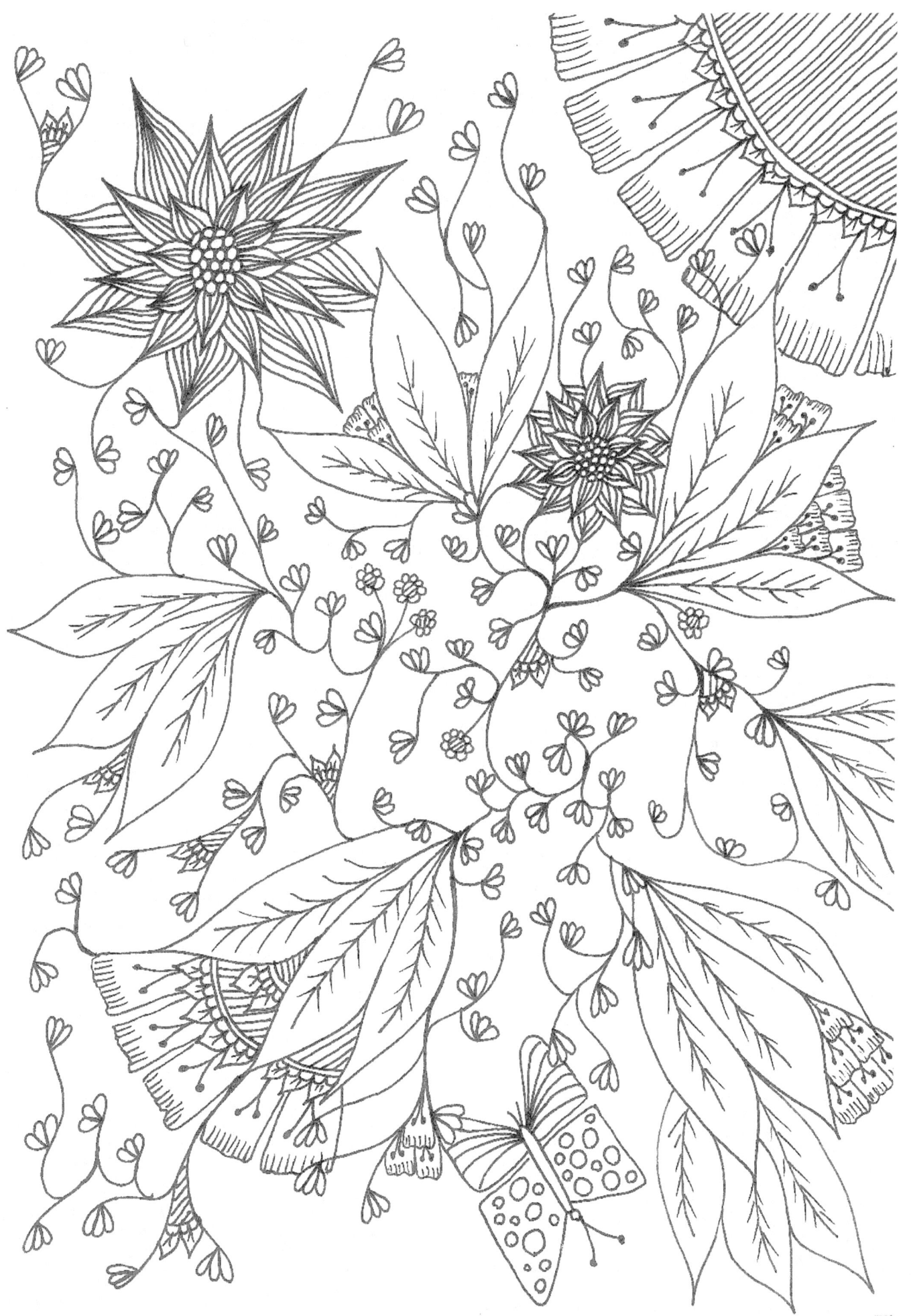

CONCLUSIONS ON A TRAIN

So I'm sat on a train to London writing the end to this book. More thinking.

Since the first book "A Working Mum's Mind" was launched, so much has happened. A new job, more kids mess to clean up, family deaths, company restructuring, holidays and lots of family celebrations. It's been incredible really and most of this has been shared with all our friends and family through social media.

Social media as a platform is categorically one of the best little inventions for communication in my opinion. It allows us to share everything with the world at the drop of a hats notice. It gives us a method to reduce time on the phone bringing everyone up to speed with what is happening in our lives and so this can only be a good thing when life is busy. Right?

Now to the flip side of this coin. On this train there is a young couple sat opposite me. They are extremely well dressed and groomed for an evening out in London. So far I think they have taken about 18 selfies and not one is good enough for the young girl. She has claimed she looks chubby, stated that his beard looks wonky, her eyelashes look too fake, her breasts don't look big enough and even that his parting is too sharp and looks ridiculous. This is the worrying part of social media for me.

They are now on selfie 22.

We all know they are going to post that photo on Instagram and create a false impression of their amazing train journey and how fabulous they look, and that false impression is what creates mess in our modern world.

They ended their selfies at 24 and the young lady has now started on her own. Number six so far.

The worst bit is that we are all a little guilty of this. In some shape or form we have all left off little details in our posts which tell the real story but across this book I hope you have seen some honesty around some of the photos that people may be posting.

I hope you have enjoyed colouring in the pages and seen the humour behind the stories.

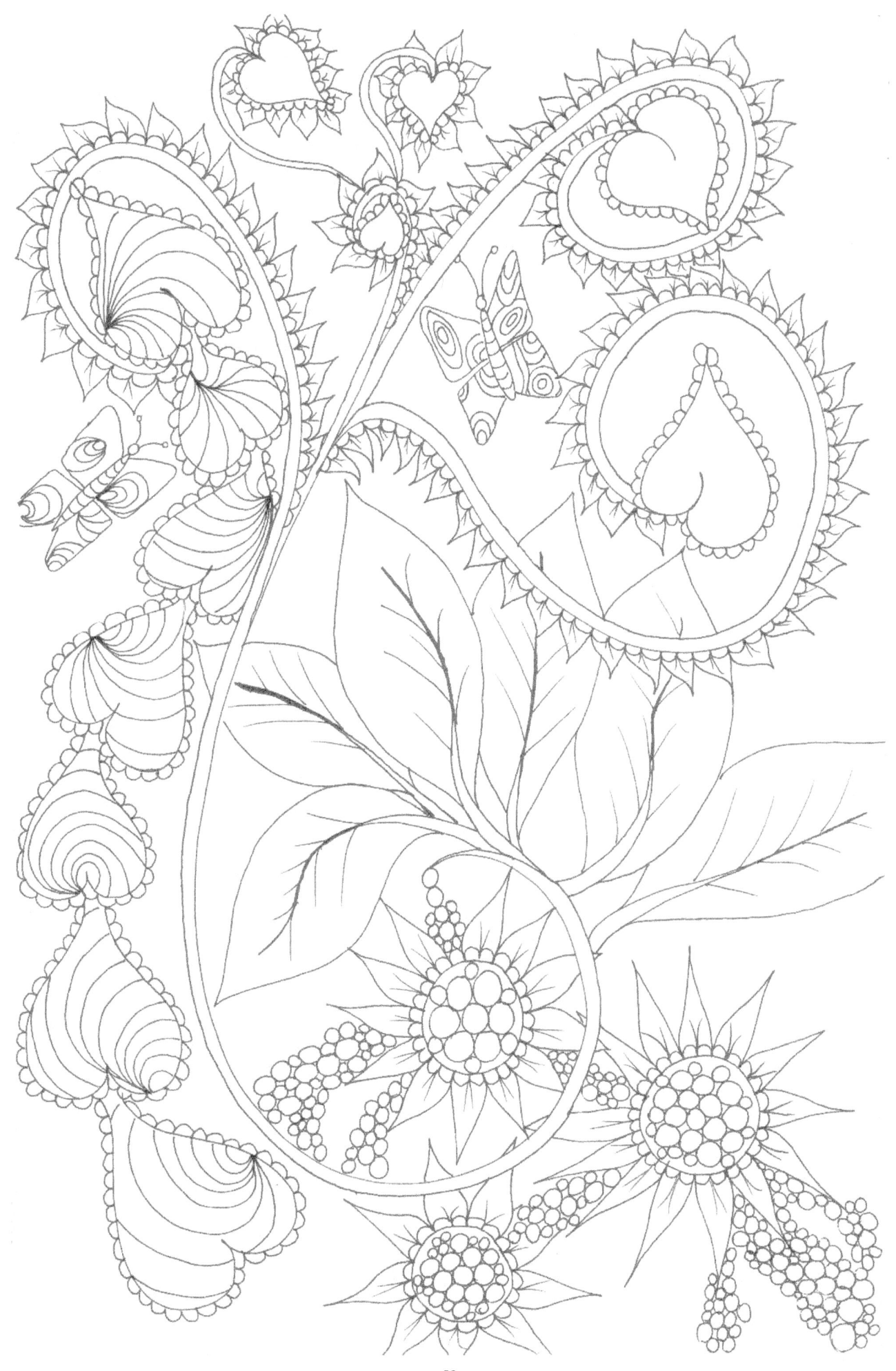

Just remember that social media is supposed to be fun. It has the word "social" in it so it's supposed to be inclusive in my little world. Don't get bogged down by comments or lack of likes. It's not worth it. This piece of wisdom is totally nicked, but I once read the below (and of course posted it). I thought it was pretty damn good:

If you had £86400 in your account and someone stole £10 from you, would you be upset and throw the remaining amount £86390 away in hopes of going back at the person who took your £10? No. You would move on and live. Right? The same way we have 86400 seconds each day. Don't let someone's negative 10 seconds ruin the remaining 86390 seconds of your day. Don't sweat the small stuff. Life is bigger than that. Have a Positive day!

Oh for god sakes!!!!! She's on selfie 14 now!! And still going......This chick is doing my head in!!!

Thank you to each and every single person who has purchased this book. The charities I am supporting, along with myself are most grateful. I would also like to say thank you to all of those people who lovingly gave me their permission to use their quotes and stories.

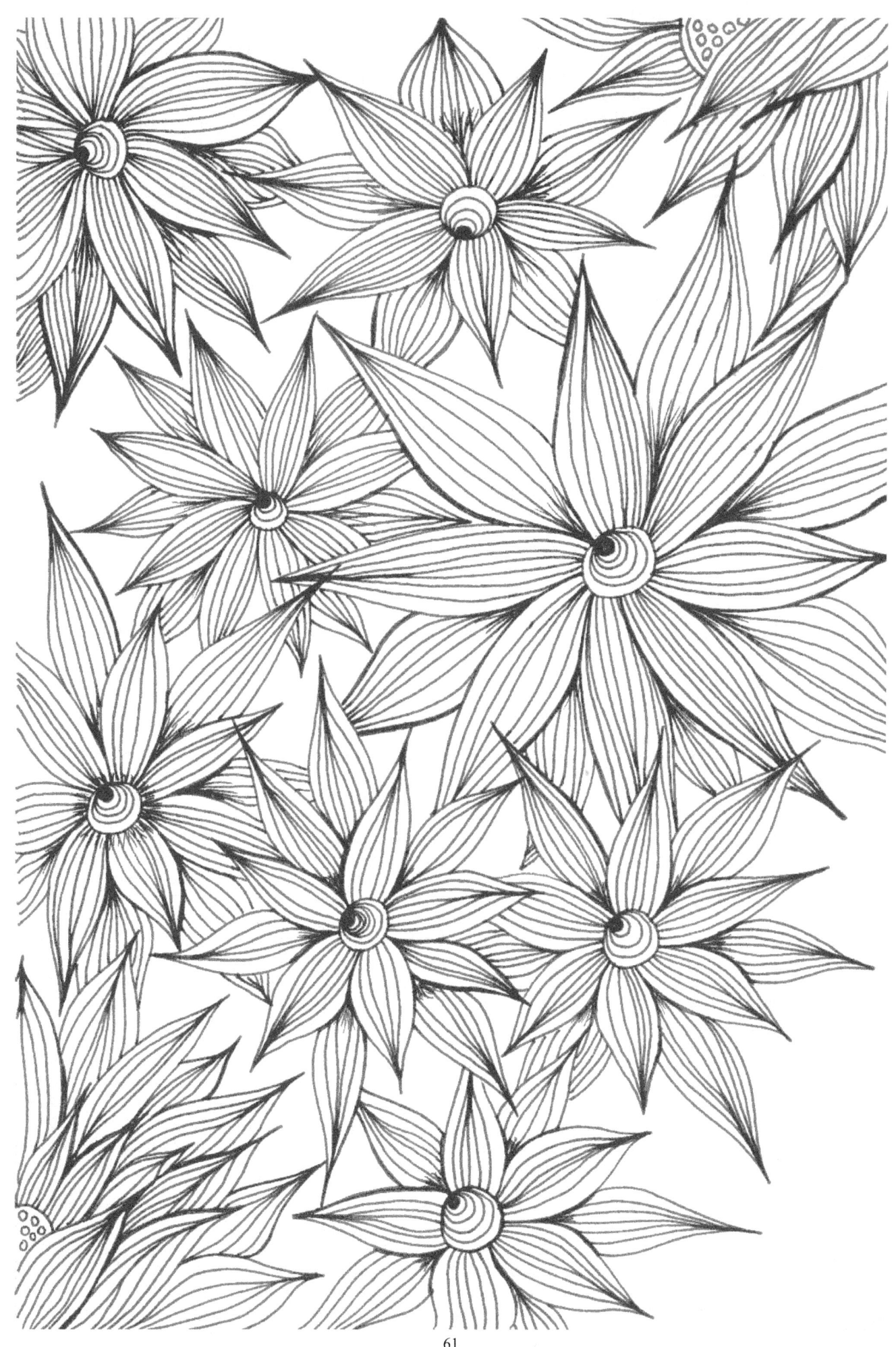